From Abuse, To

Edited By

April Gamble, Sherrell McCullough, Christy Murray

CONTENTS

CHAPTER 1.. Elementary

CHAPTER 2..Teenager

CHAPTER 3..High School

CHAPTER 4..Meeting Him

CHAPTER 5..Getting To Know Him

CHAPTER 6..........................On Our Way To Start Our Future

CHAPTER 7..My King Was Born

CHAPTER 8..My Second King Was Born

CHAPTER 9... I Was Not The only One Going Through Hell

CHAPTER 10..The Last Straw

CHAPTER 11..On Our Way To The Land

CHAPTER 12..Who Am I

CHAPTER 13..Reality Check

CHAPTER 14..Get It Together Angelica

CHAPTER 15..Show Time

CHAPTER 16..........................If You Knew Better You Do Better

CHAPTER 17...............Loyalty Sometimes Gets You Nowhere

CHAPTER 18...Moving Forward

CHAPTER 19..Found Love

CHAPTER 20...The Turn Around

CHAPTER 21..I'm A Rider

CHAPTER 22............................Time I Get Me Together

CHAPTER 23...........................Grind Time

CHAPTER 24............................You Can And You Will

INTRODUCTION

This book was written to inform not only women but also men too, that You Can and You Will conquer anything life throws at you. You just have to believe. This book talks about many obstacles and life experiences I've gone through; "Little did I know that's just a part of life." Unfortunately, I wanted so badly and even attempted giving up sometimes. However, as time went on and looking at the hurt in my children's eyes; It helped motivate me to try to do better and to be better. Life is filled with obstacles. We just have to learn how to overcome them.

You Can and You Will

Chapter 1

Elementary

It was 1986, and at the age of five, Mommy was picking out my hair like an Afro and spraying curl spray in it. I hated my mother putting curls in my hair. She would just spray my hair and pick it out. I guess it was convenient for her because she worked a lot of double shifts to make ends meet she had nine mouths to feed, including daddy's mouth. Although Dad worked too, mommy worked first shift sometimes and even double shifts to make ends meet. On my way to school I would cry because the kids would call me Janet Jackson. Sometimes I just wanted to crawl under a rock. I hardly had any friends. My clothes were falling off of me because they were my big sister's clothes. I was picked on in school because what I looked like. "My appearance was not the best".

I struggled in school with the material. I didn't do well in Math, so I cheated because I didn't have anyone to show me how to add or subtract. In first grade, a friend of mine by the name of Steve showed me how to add and subtract in class. My clothes were barely washed because mom worked so much she never had the time. Not trying to take from her, but her hands were full with working, cooking, and just trying to take care of a whole household of ten.

My best friend stayed next door, her name was Arial. Arial's mom would give me Arial's clothes, which I was so happy to receive, although they were big because Arial was taller than me. I was just so happy to get them because they were so pretty. If it were not for Sam, Arial's Mom, I would not have known what water parks looked like, bowling, skating, going out to eat and seeing fireworks every year. Not taking anything from my mom because she was doing her best taking care of nine kids.

My parents did not have the time and they didn't have the money either. We ate chicken, beans, and cornbread every day. OMG I hate beans! Monday was Lima beans. Tuesday was chilly. Wednesday was butter beans, chicken, and corn bread. Thursday maybe we got lucky and got to eat spaghetti; eating pasta was a privilege in our house. Friday, whatever left overs we had, Daddy would mix it up together and that was our meal.

I remember racing downstairs in the morning to get a spoon, because we only had so many spoons. The first three to get to the kitchen was the first to eat cereal. The rest would have to wait, or eat with a fork. We sat at a long table in the dining room but we didn't have enough chairs to sit at the table so we sat on the benches daddy used to workout on and crates that were stolen from the corner store. Me being so small I had to stack the crates to reach the table.

It was a big house, just was not the cleanest. The roaches were so bad that you would be watching TV and they would crawl across the TV, but soon as you got up to smack them down, you they would run inside the TV. The only friends that I really had had been the ones that stayed on the streets. So I was not ashamed of them to come over and see the roaches, they were used to them. Those friends would be racing to help kill them when they saw any run across the floor.

However, I was embarrassed to let any other company come over. I shared my bedroom with five of my sisters. Oh yes! I had five sisters and three brothers! And, a brother; my Mom had a son before she and my dad got together. I never slept in a bed alone as a child, but I was okay with that because I liked sharing a bed with my sisters.

There were some strange things going at my house some nights. My parents would let all kinds of family stay with us, which included cousins and uncles. Whoever was in the family needed a place to stay was welcomed at our house. My parents were very helpful when it came to other people needing a place to stay. They always opened their door. Some nights the opposite sex would get in the bed with me or I saw one maybe lay next to my sister a year older than me, which was Amanda. I would just lay there in fear too scared to move. Some of the things that happened I knew should not have been done to her. I tried blocking some things out, because I knew some things were just not right.

Although Holiday times were the best, we might not had much but we had each other. We were like, "The Ghetto Cosby Show," especially on Mom and Dad's anniversary. My big sisters would cook for them. My Dad was hard on us, but he was the glue that held the family together. We would get together and sing and dance for my parents. My oldest brother, Paul, would rap because he was very talented with music and he could sing to.

My oldest sister, Kaylee, was talented as well. She had the most beautiful voice you could hear. The rest of us would just crack jokes and perform for mommy and daddy by dancing, which was my talent. I loved dancing. Before the night was over, Mom and Dad would hand dance. I loved watching them hand dance in the middle of the floor and we would all surround them dancing with each other.

One time, my dad's brother who was my favorite uncle threw a party in the basement and daddy had him to come get me so I could dance in front of everyone. I wasn't scared because he promised to buy me a new pair of shoes. I was excited! I went downstairs and did the "Cabbage Patch Dance," and they all stood around me dancing, saying things like, "get it baby." The next day my uncle Scott took me to get a new pair of shoes. A lot of us looked up to Uncle Scott because he was so cool.

Uncle Scott was very helpful and intelligent. We all loved him because he was so genuine. Uncle Scott and daddy were very close. He was always there when daddy needed him. I was so happy. I didn't have to wear those blue rubber shoes I got from school anymore just because I did the happy dance. We would do the same for Christmas. We would all dance and perform for mommy and daddy, although, I didn't get many presents. It didn't matter. We had each other. Back then it was better than getting a lot of toys.

My older sister, Heaven, would buy me presents because either she knew I was not going to get much or she just wanted to because she had such a great heart. Heaven took me to get my first ear piercing. I love Heaven she was a sweet person. Everyone loved her. I was so grateful for what I had and was glad to be around family. Sometimes I would get sad when Arial would show me her toys, but glad she would allow me to play with them. My Birthday was on Christmas Eve. I never had a party; my parents would always say, "Christmas is the next day." So a lot of times I didn't get a gift for my birthday because of that. I did not understand back then that my parents had eight other children and that it would be a bit much for them.

Chapter 2

Teenager

In 1993, by the age of twelve, my sisters started moving out and my mother had us join a Baptist Church on 93rd Street off of Miles. I loved that church. Everyone there was really nice to us. She would always teach us about God, talk about him and how we should be good to others. We were Baptist, and went to church sometimes three days a week. Sunday was church, Wednesday was Bible Study, and Thursday was choir practice. Oh yes! We had to sing in the choir too! I couldn't sing worth a crap! I tried. My parents made us go to church faithfully. I remember hiding my shoes some mornings so I didn't have to go. Daddy would say, "no church, no going outside!" So I would go act like I found them so I could go outside after church.

It was my sister Amanda's birthday and she was having a party. We had some neighborhood friends over such as: Ashley, Arial, Sadie, and some of Amanda's friends. I remember my sisters and brothers making fun of me. That's the thing; cracking jokes were big in our family. They cracked jokes on everyone, but when they got to me they would sing and joke "A is for Apple, J is for Jack, Angelica aint got no hair in the back."

I instantly got sad because I felt embarrassed. Everyone was laughing! So I struck after one of my sisters that were making fun of me as if I could beat her. My Dad came over and told me "you don't be trying to fight your sister!" He smacked me so hard I saw sparks and I fainted! I woke up and saw Ashley standing over me, asking me if I was ok. I was so embarrassed after that. When I woke up my face was numb. I ran upstairs crying. This was not the first time I had blacked out when my father hit me. A Couple of times I was choked and thrown up the stairs.

My father was no joke, he loved us very much, but he was a no nonsense type of man. He did not play! If you cut up or did something you knew you were not supposed to have done, that was your ass! If you got a whooping by him he would put his size 13's on your backside! Sometimes we would try to put layers of clothes on and he said, "I don't whoop clothes I bought". So we would get whooping's in our undies. I tried my best to stay out of trouble.

My brother Paul was one of the biggest drug dealers on Lee Road; "up the way" they would call it. He would come in and out of the house with all this flashy jewelry. He had cars with switches on them back then it was big. He also had motorcycles. You could hear him coming home on his bikes from a mile away. It would be him and about forty other bikes riding along side of him. I looked up to my brother Paul. He had it going on.

I didn't know how he was getting all these nice things, until one day he was on a high-speed chase from the police and he ran up to me while I was sitting on our front porch. He then gave me a clear bag that looked like a sandwich bag with white looking rocks. I felt nervous. I had a feeling something wasn't right. He took off running and they couldn't catch him of course. He was a fast runner. He then ran back to the house and grabbed it from me.

Paul had so much money at the time. His so called friends one time kicked our front door in and put a gun to my mother's head and Paul's girlfriend Kristy's head and asked them to go in the basement to show them where he was hiding his money. No one was home but mommy, Kristy and Granddad, and Granddad was sick. He was asleep in the back room and slept through the entire ordeal, which was a good thing because he was crazy. Of course they kicked the door in after Amanda and I went to school. When Arial came to school that's when I found out what had happened. She told me because she was late getting to school. I left immediately scared and nervous.

Paul was really into rapping and dancing. My older sister Kaylee could sing and hit Whitney Houston notes so well! She also liked modeling. She then tried to further her singing and modeling career and in doing so, got caught up with the wrong crowd. She got caught up in that street life style. She had a child who stayed with us also, by the name of Brooklyn. Brooklyn is two years younger than I am.

Brooklyn would try and fight with all my friends all the time. My neighborhood friend, Kerry, was my best friend. She lived down the street from me. Although I did not have friends in school, I had neighborhood friends. I had a friend by the name of Ashley who was the sister of Paul's girlfriend Kristy. She was so fun and she loved dancing just like me. We would make up dance routines and her sister, Kristy, would always take us out to the skating rink so we could dance.

At that time I knew I loved dancing. We would turn the school dances out as well. Meanwhile, I started liking boys. My appearance still wasn't too good, but thanks to Ashley and a great friend I've known since I was like 6 years old, the two of them helped me get my appearance together. Kerry used to let me wear her clothes in Junior High School. She and Ashley used to comb my hair. But I still didn't have too many guys that liked me. I had a crush on one guy, and he loved dancing as well. His name was Michael. He was always my dancing partner at the school dances.

Junior High Graduation came! Wow! I was getting ready for High School. I begged my mother to let me go with her to pick out my graduation outfit. My friends were bragging about what kind of outfit they were getting. Daddy went and got my sister Amanda and I outfits. Amanda was a year older than me. One day Daddy came back with karate looking suits from Value City. I kind of felt bad because he was so happy he went and picked them out but I felt like crying because they looked like Karate suits. I cried my butt off because I felt like I was going to a Karate class. Especially when I knew my friend's outfits were so pretty.

After graduation summer came and I landed myself a summer job at the age of fifteen. I knew if I could get a summer job, I could have a good chance of buying clothes for High School so I could look nice and fit in. At least that's what I was thinking. I told Amanda, "you know Mommy and Daddy are only going to get us two to three outfits a piece at the most, so let's get a summer job."

Amanda said, "No, I want to be able to play for the summer." I said, "Ok." Yes, I spent all of my checks on clothes and for High School! I bought shoes and jewelry. Tommy Hilfiger and Nautica was the thing at the time. Because I was Ninety-six pounds my shoe size was a four. I shopped at Dillard's in the kid's section; therefore, I was able to buy twice as much.

Chapter 3

High School

In 1996, my freshman year at Kennedy High School I made it on the High Stepping Team. They called me "Baby Baller" when I got to High School because I had a lot of nice clothes and shoes. Paul had bought me a herringbone and I had bought myself some rings back when everyone was wearing Mickey Mouse rings. I was finally fitting in! Yes! I was so happy, until Daddy decided to retire from the Post Office and move to Alabama. I was thinking to myself, "NO, this can't be! I just started fitting in and I have more friends. This can't be happening to me!"

My Father went down to Alabama to visit; so we thought, but when he came home, he told Mommy he no longer wanted to stay in Cleveland especially since our door got kicked in and Mommy had a gun put to her head. Of course my Mother did not want to move back down to Alabama. My Dad moved her away from there many years ago. She had a past I knew nothing about at the time. My mother ran away at the age of twelve because her stepfather kept raping and beating her and her sister. After my mother ran away she later met my father. He had just gotten out of Vietnam. He later moved her to Cleveland. After she left Alabama she later sent for her siblings as well. Daddy told Mommy that we had to leave, and that we had to leave in less than a month. Mommy never wanted to move back there because of her past. She told my father she didn't want to move back and he knew her past, but he told her he was going still. I think too much was going on when my brother's friends kicked the door in and put the gun to mommy's head. After that, Daddy wanted to leave the city. So she made her mind up to follow her husband. I was so sad to leave my friends. We cried together. I did not want to go, Mommy took me to say goodbye to Ashley and Kerry, and that was the saddest day for me. Looking out the window, waving goodbye was so hard for me. I cried almost the entire ride to Alabama. Daddy came later and brought the rest of our things.

As we pulled into Brent, Alabama, I was thinking to myself, I so do not want to be here right now. There were no sidewalks and a lot of red dirt. Although I was amazed about how much land my Dad had bought. Daddy ran out to give us hugs and to show us our home. It was really nice compared to where we had come from, but it was not home. My Dad later introduced Amanda and I to two girls by the names of Alexis and Sabrina. They were my cousins who were really nice. We all went to school together, they told me they loved dancing too. We clicked pretty well and we all had beautiful shapes. I had just started showing my shape at the beginning of High School.

The first day of school, girls were looking at me as if to say, "Who is this city girl?" Guys were rushing to ask my cousins Alexis and Sabrina to figure out who is this new girl? I clicked with my cousins Sabrina and Alexis right away. Sabrina was like a little sister to me, we clicked right away, and we had become really close. Sabrina was fun, and sometimes laid back but she could be a firecracker if you pissed her off! Alexis was like my big sister she was filled with so much life and energy. Everyone loved to be around her. Those that didn't like Alexis knew not to fuck with her. She was known for whooping ass, but she had a big heart, with an ass a mile long. Oh yes, we Carter girls were known for our shapes. I loved spending the night at their house, and I tried to go over there every weekend. The females did not like that at all.

One day in school a young lady approached me and asked me if I had been talking about her. I told her, "I don't even know you and I could care less." I smiled and as I walked away she hit me. The next thing I knew was that we were fighting! I was cut on my face but I didn't care. My sister Jackie came up to the school in a rage. Jackie had moved down to Alabama after we did. When I returned home my dad told me, "you better go back to school and you better whoop her ass."

I was so angry that I had to get three stitches. When I went back to school I snuck a blade into the school. My intentions were to cut her on her face as payback. I was filled with rage because I didn't bother anyone. All I remember was that the guards couldn't hold me back. I was expelled from school and from then on I had to go to summer school in Tuscaloosa so I wouldn't be held back.

I later met two close friends named Maria and Tonya. They were both from Chicago. Maria and Tonya were fun, especially Tonya. She brought out the wild side in me. Tonya was fun and wild. I loved it though. Maria was fun but more laid back, and we were like sisters. We thought alike. I loved kicking it with the two of them because they were both nice and they loved to dance like me. I was shocked that we had so much in common while living down south. I still kept in contact with my friends from up north. So much was going on up there.

I heard that my niece Brooklyn ended up getting on drugs. Her father, I was told, introduced this to her. Brooklyn was like my little sister. I took her with me everywhere. It really hurt me to find out she was going down the wrong road. I wish she could have moved down South with us, but she had to stay with her mom in Cleveland.

 Arial ended up doing different things. Ashley began to live a different lifestyle because she was going through some things up there and later got her life back on track. At the time, I was kind of relieved because I had no clue where I would've been had I still been up there. Although, I was still missing my friends and family, the only friend that seemed to be doing well was Kerry.

Chapter 4

Meeting Him

In the meantime, down South I was at a house party with my cousins Alexis and Sabrina. A guy by the name of Rocky comes up to me and asks me my name. The first thing that went through my head is, "OMG this guy looks like a wolf!" I was not interested at all! Someone told me he was 21 years old. Mind you I was only 16. It was the summer of 1997. He was very aggressive by following me around all over the party. He told me I was going to be his wife, and that I would have his children. That really wasn't attractive to me. I was kind of freaked out by that.

My cousins Alexis, Sabrina, my friend Steve, and my sister Amanda had all gone to a party two weeks later, and it were packed. Rocky was there, and by that time I had started thinking twice about him. I was thinking to myself, "maybe he's not that bad." He was sending balloons and flowers to my school. He would pop up after school and ask me if I wanted a ride home. I was thinking to myself, "he seemed ok I guess." I never had a guy buy me shoes, send me flowers and always doing things for me. I felt like he swept me off my feet. Months went by and Rocky and I started getting closer. I had to sneak around with him because of his age. He used to hang out with my male cousins, so that was like my play off.

One day he and I were together, he started kissing me all over my body. My heart started racing and I started thinking to myself, "OMG I don't know if I'm ready for this." He told me to relax, and that he loved me and wanted to be with me for the rest of his life. After we had sex, and I lost my virginity, he told me I was his forever. At that time I didn't know what to think. Later, I started hearing he was engaged and had a child on the way, but that was before my time. It was hard for me to believe because he was always with me but I was so young and I didn't really know what to think. Nevertheless, I had to question him about it. He said it was true but that he didn't love her anymore, and that he was leaving her. I had all kinds of mixed feelings about that. I told him not to, and that he should stay with her. He claimed he didn't want to, and that he was not happy. I felt bad because I was told she was a great person.

So I later found out that he was with both of us. He then left her and I started hearing rumors about him beating and jumping on her. I questioned him about it and he denied it, of course. As time went by, Rocky started getting jealous of the clothes that I was wearing. He would say, "I don't want you wearing tight clothes anymore." He would say it made me look like a hoe, which was definitely a red flag. I was very shapely and he hated to see other guys looking at me. He didn't like the attention I was getting. I didn't really think much of it at the time. When you are young you just don't know any better and some may even think it's cute to have someone who cares and gives you that kind of attention; not knowing or seeing the signs of control.

Chapter 5

Getting to Know Him

My senior year came. By this time, I was not allowed to have any male friends. Rocky started grabbing my arms tight if I did anything he didn't approve of which later developed into him pushing me. Everyone was scared to be my friend because of him. He had a reputation of fighting a lot. He loved fighting. He would try to fight anyone that tried to get close to me, including females. So, my senior year was pretty lonely for me. I loved him, but I felt like I had no life! He would ask me to marry him but every time he did, I would say, "no." I wanted to go to college with my best friend Kerry because we had always promised to go to college together.

I took drama classes in High School because I always knew I wanted to be an actress. Every since I was a child putting on shows for my family was something I loved to do. I loved movies. I could watch movies all day if I could. Drama, Horror, Comedy, and western, I loved them all. Unfortunately, there was a time Rocky asked me to marry him and I said, "no," which lead to him drinking rat poison. Rocky said if he couldn't have me then didn't want to live. I didn't know what to do. I was 18 years old! I felt scared and sad at the same time. I felt bad for him. I wanted to help him but I did not know how. I told him after they released him from the psych ward that I would marry him.

Obviously, I was not thinking clearly because Rocky had problems. But I also told him we would have to move back to Ohio because I did not want to stay in Alabama after school. He was so excited. I was scared inside not knowing what I was getting myself into. I did not know how to explain this move to my best friend and that I would not be going to college with her. Not only were our future plans ruined, but also our plans to be reunited became unlikely. I felt as if I let her down.

Friday was the day we were supposed to get married. I was nervous about marrying him all that day while I was in school. All of a sudden I was called on the PA to come to the office. I get up out of my chair thinking, "what could this be about?" So I walked to the office and it was Rocky standing outside the door with flowers. As I approached him, he asked me if I was still going to marry him. You would've thought I would've have been happy but that made me a little more nervous; another red flag that I ignored. I was so worried as I answered yes nervously. He was very happy. He kissed me and said; "I'll see you later."

After school we got married at the courthouse. We had a BBQ to celebrate afterwards. My father asked me before I married, "Are you sure this is what you want to do?" I said "yes," but I was unsure truthfully. So my dad said, "I'm behind you in whatever you want to do."

Chapter 6

On Our Way To Start Our Future

After the wedding the abuse started slowly. We moved to Canton, Ohio, which is where he was from. I did not know a soul from that town. He had a lot of family from there. Later on, he would start putting his hands around my neck if I did something he thought was stupid, or something he did not like. Then I found out I was pregnant. I talked to some cousins of his about going to college in the area because I wanted to go to college. But I never followed through.

We stayed with his grandmother while looking for a home for us. While staying there, I saw a side of him that scared me. He started coming home drunk at night, yet another red Flag. Some nights he wouldn't come home until the next morning. I would cry all night. One night he did not come home nor did he call the next morning. I instantly got scared. I later received a phone call from Rocky stating he was in jail. I cried so badly. Here I am pregnant in a town where I didn't know anyone! His family loved me and they were really nice, but I just felt alone. I would go visit him every week so he knew I was there for him. I would even write the judge apologizing just in case he could come home to his family early.

As time went by I started getting too big to fit into my clothes. Rocky's Grandmother would take me to buy clothes. I didn't have any money of course because I was on welfare, which was my only benefit at the time. I really loved his Grandmother. I would fall asleep in the bed with her watching "Nick at Night" all the time. She was really nice to me, and she treated me like I was family, but I was still lonely and confused out there. I had no family there. They sentenced Rocky to six months in jail. So, I called my family in Cleveland, which was 45 minutes away. They came and picked me up. I stayed with my sister Sarah, who I thought had the perfect family. Rocky was not happy with my leaving, he wanted me to stay with his family. We bonded great. I got a job at Subway because the welfare checks were not enough. The good thing was, I felt like I needed to be doing something until the Doctor told me to quit. Unfortunately, I started having problems during the pregnancy because I was high risk. Although this man was mean to me I still loved him. Cheating on him wouldn't have even cross my mind. I still stuck by his side.

    I bonded well with Sarah when I stayed with her. She was very comforting and uplifting. She was very supportive. Six months came to an end; it was time for Rocky to get out. I caught the bus back to Canton to pick Rocky up from jail. We stayed a couple nights then we went back to Cleveland. My stomach was really big by this time. We thought staying in Ohio would not be a good idea for us; I was too scared he would get into trouble again. The plan was to have my father pick us up from my sister's house and move back to Alabama. He told me we wouldn't have a life up north because he would stay in trouble. So I thought it was best to move back down South; although I did not want to go back, but I did it for him.

He mentally abused me when we came back to Cleveland. He would say, "You're not a good wife because you left me in Canton." I told him I just wanted to be with my family. He called me a hoe and other names. He said I was out here cheating on him, which was a lie. I cried so badly. I repeated, "I love you, and I never slept with any other men!" I also told him, "I didn't want anyone else I only wanted you, I waited on you, but that wasn't enough!" We waited on my father to come get us for about a week. In the meantime, he worked with my sister's husband who was an electrician. He showed Rocky how to do electrician work. He showed him the works. So he did odd jobs to make money until my father came and got us. I gave my father one hundred dollars to come get us.

So back down South we went. I was kind of sad, but my Mother always taught me to follow your husband, so I did. When we got back down South, Rocky continued to mentally and physically abuse me. When we got back to Alabama, I stayed with my parents until I got my own apartment, which was a few months after I got there. Then I landed a job at Pizza Hut as a waitress/cashier. He then found a job at Wal-Mart stocking shelves. He showed the company that was remodeling Wal-Mart; he knew how to do electrical work as well. So he then landed an electrician job. They tried to pay for him to go to school to get his license so he can make even more money. Even though he was making decent money with that company, he had drinking problems and couldn't keep a steady job.

Chapter 7

My King Was Born

January 22, 2001, I had my first son Jacob. I was happy but I didn't feel like I was ready to be a mother. I didn't know how. I wanted to go to college. All I know is that I wanted to be one out of nine kids to go to College. I wanted to be someone. Not saying that the others were not. Well, I had one sister that attended college. There was something about when I held Jacob in my arms that gave me a feeling I could not explain. It was a strong bond and love. I came home from the hospital tired and remembered Rocky leaving me home with the baby to run the streets. I cried I was so depressed. I was so tired. I felt like I needed some rest and some help, and all he wanted to do was run the streets.

I gained some weight and the abuse became stronger. He would call me fat. He wouldn't even want to sleep in the bed with me for months at a time. I felt worthless, unattractive, and ugly. He told me nobody would love me like he did. He would say, "You're too fat to have sex with and you also have ugly stretch marks." Some nights I would just cry myself to sleep. I would think and wish I could be small again so he would want me again. Mind you I was little all of my life until I had a child. The most I ever weighed was 116 lbs., but I had gotten up to 135lbs after birth. So I was really feeling some kind of way. I felt like crap.

The coming home drunk became worse because I was not allowed to have any friends nor hang out with my cousins anymore. I became really lonely. So going to work was an escape for me. There were even times I went to work with a black eye. I didn't even care; I just wanted to get out of that house. I wanted to work every day if it was possible. My niece Angel would always keep my son and watch him for me while I worked. She was named after me.

She was like my stepdaughter; I kept her with me at all times. Mind you I didn't drink nor smoke, so my only getaway was work. Rocky wouldn't let anyone come around me that smoked or drank. I had no one I could call. I was too scared to bring anyone around. No one wanted to keep hearing what I was going through and I kept going back to him, so I thought. So I just kept everything to myself and held everything in.

One day I was sitting on our porch and Rocky started another job at the Lumber Mill ten minutes away from the house. A couple of female neighbors were sitting on the porch with me, which were people I had gone to school with. They were really nice to me. I was just excited to have someone to talk to. He walks up and starts calling me fat names. He made them leave. After they left he jumped on me. He told me I wasn't allowed to have any friends.

He said he was the only friend I needed and that everyone else was not my real friend, that they were fake. I was only allowed to wear big clothes at this time. So I found myself wearing his clothes. By this time I had given up on my appearances. I stopped combing my hair. I felt torn down! After my friends had left, he jumped on me and starting beating me. I just went in the room and balled up and cried. All I could think is that I never met someone that could hate their wife so much and be so mean to someone that they loved. I thought to myself, "This can't be marriage and that I never witnessed this type of behavior with my parents." I couldn't do anything but hope and pray things would get better with time.

The next morning I woke up with a sore body and I was crying, I was too embarrassed to face the two young ladies that were over at my house when that happened. He took the house phone when he went to work so I wouldn't call anyone. I was getting tired of him jumping on me. I left him and went to my mother's house. When he got off work, he came and he was begging me to come home.

I said to him, "you need some help." I said I could no longer do this because I felt so worthless. He promised he'd get help. He also said he just feared me leaving him. He said his father left him when he was five and his mom was not around often as a child. I told him he had problems and he needed to get help if he wanted me to come home. So I came home and he was good for about a week. Than the abuse started again. He never did seek help!

Chapter 8

My Second King Was Born

Months went by and I found out I was pregnant again. I cried my but off because I was not ready for another child. I already had too many problems. I felt like a single mother when it came to taking care of our kids. I was drained, both mentally and physically. Rocky was a great provider financially, but I was up all day and night with Jacob. Rocky never really had time for Jacob. He would play with him when he came home for a minute than he'd be gone.

I think I cried for about two weeks because I knew he wouldn't be there to help me. I'd be raising two kids alone. He'd rather be in the streets instead of being home helping me. Don't get me wrong, he would work to take care of us financially, he just didn't want to put in quality time. He was in the streets all the time doing whatever it was he was doing.

August 13, 2002, Jayden was born. Although I was not ready for another child again when I held Jayden there was a bond, love that was unexplainable. Things didn't get better. In fact, they got worse. I started hearing rumors that he was snorting cocaine on top of already being a heavy drinker. I asked him about it and he got mad and said, "no." "Who said that he asked?" I never told him! One night his friend Jack and his fiancé came over. Her name was Bella. They were drinking and watching TV. While I was cooking I was talking to Bella in the kitchen. We were talking about "women" things. After we all ate dinner we were sitting in the living room just talking.

All of a sudden Rocky starts cursing me out because Bella asked me to sip on some coolers with her. He flips out so they felt uncomfortable and started getting ready to go. Bella put on her coat and I went outside behind her begging her not to leave. I asked her to stay. I was scared he was going to jump on me. But I didn't know how to tell her that. He came outside accusing me of being gay, saying to me, "why are you outside with her?" I said to him, "I'm not gay," feeling embarrassed.

So I went back in the house and Jack was using the bathroom. He came out and said he'd see us later and thanked me for the dinner. After Jack left Rocky started punching me. I was holding my oldest son Jacob in my arms. I asked him why are you hitting me I didn't do anything wrong! I fell to the floor and then Rocky started stomping on me! I thought to myself he's going to kill me. I was terrified!

I heard a knocking at the door and it was Jack. He forgot his jacket. I thought to myself, "I've got to get out of here, he's going to kill me." So I grabbed Jacob and Jayden and ran out of the house to Bella's car. I said crying, "please take me to my mother's house, he just jumped on me for no reason!" I was shaking and terrified. Jayden and Jacob just had on pampers and sleepers. The look on her face was puzzled like she was in shock. She said, "Okay, I'll take you." She dropped me off and went back to get Jack 20-30 minutes later. It didn't dawn on me that he would be mad when she came back to get Jack. I was just trying to hurry up and get out of there.

Bella walked in my mother's door with a bloody face. Blood was coming all down the side of her face. The back of her neck had blood running all down it. Rocky was behind her holding a gun to the back of her head saying to her, "You took my wife away from me!" She looked terrified. She was crying as she walked into the house. I instantly dialed 911 shaking and screaming. My father was sitting in his chair and he told Rocky to "get his ass out of his house." I felt a little secure but I didn't know what he was going to try to do next. He ran out. I started crying when I saw all the blood running down her face. I felt it was entirely my fault he jumped on her. If only I'd told her not to go back up there and to have Jack meet her somewhere else. I was not thinking clearly.

I thought to myself, "this was entirely your fault." Had she not helped me, none of this would've happened. I ended up taking Bella to the hospital. She had to have 14 stitches. He busted her front windshield while she was driving him to me. She said Rocky had beaten her with his gun while she was trying to break him up from fighting Jack.

Rocky was angry saying to her, " you took my wife away from me." Jack got between them trying to calm him down, Rocky then jumped on Jack with the gun. He was hitting him in the head with the gun. So when Bella tried to tell him to stop he started jumping on her, that's when he made her drive him to my mother's house to find me. I felt so bad for Bella. Bella had to press charges on Rocky. I then left Rocky for a while after that had happened; I was terrified that I didn't know the man that was in my bed. I was sleeping with a stranger.

The next morning I remember going back to the house to get clothes for the babies. Jackie and I went to get some things for the babies, diapers, clothes and milk. I remember Jackie running out of the kids' room. I knew at that moment he was there. Jackie started pointed silently saying, "He's in the closet." She took off running and I took off after her. I ran so fast out of the house that when it was time to turn the corner I couldn't turn because I was running so fast. He was in the boys' closet hiding with clothes over top of him so when she moved the clothes she said she saw something moving. I guess he thought we were the police. I stayed with my parents because I was too afraid to go back to that house. He was hiding out from the police.

Chapter 9

I Was Not the Only One Going Through Hell

So much was going on outside of my marriage. My brother Paul ended up coming down South. Paul went from being the biggest dope dealer to a user. It hurt me to death to see him like that. I cried so much for a while. I begged him to stop, and I did not understand why he did this. I told him that I loved him so much and that I used to look up to him, but it didn't help. It crushed me to see him like that. I would pray that he would stop, but nope! He was stealing from my parents and breaking into stores at the same time. So much was going on at my parent's house. Paul was putting them through a lot. Between myself and my mother's other children, she ended up running away from home without telling us. I guess "she" couldn't deal with all that was going on any longer.

I later found out that my father used to fight with my mother. I, however, never witnessed that. It stopped when I was coming up as a child. I guess that scared my mom, me going through what she went through. Mommy left driving to Cleveland, I think she was trying to get to Sarah, whom is my sister that lives in Cleveland, but she didn't make it, mom crashed in Columbus, Ohio. Mommy was trying to get away from all the drama that was going on in Alabama. On top of Mommy losing her sister, whom she was really close with. My mother had several siblings but she was really close to the one that past. They had the same father you see, my mother ran away at the age 12 years old.

My mother was tired of being raped by her stepfather. He would come into her bedroom and rape her and my Aunt that passed. He was her sisters and brothers father. So they had been through a lot together. She told me he used to come in their room and put a knife to her neck and rape her and her sister. My mother never got help for what happened. She just buried it. My mother ran away because she got tired of it. She never made it to High School because she had her first child at 14 years old. She worked two jobs so that she could provide for her family.

A couple of years later she met my father. He had just come back from Vietnam. They dated for a while then they got married. I am going to go back to the part where my mother crashed her car in Columbus for a moment. Well, she totaled it. My father picked her up and brought her back home. She had a couple of bruises but she was able to walk away from it. Thank God! I felt so bad about that. I felt like it was my fault. I felt like I was part of the reason she left. She later had a nervous breakdown. They locked her up in a psych ward. I didn't understand. I was hurt, and I knew my mom was not crazy. I wanted them to let her out. It hurt me when I went to see her. They doped her up and she was like a zombie. I cried for nights and nights. I hated to see her that way.

Meanwhile, Rocky had heard this and tried to come back. I needed a shoulder to cry on. He was really all I knew, and he was very happy I needed him again. He was there for me so I went back to him. They diagnosed my mother with schizophrenia. My father had her admitted because he said he couldn't handle her. I was so confused because after I took Rocky back he went back to his old ways. I felt clueless as to why was I going through so much. I wanted out so badly, but I was afraid of leaving and raising my kids alone. I wanted my children to have a father in the house as I did as a child. But little did I know my situation was not healthy and that we were better off alone.

One day I got tired of sitting at home. I wanted to get out of the house. So I went over to my Auntie's house where my little cousin DJ was staying. I had my niece Angel babysit the boys for me while I stepped out of the house to go hang with DJ. DJ was like my little sister; we were real close growing up. My dad used to take DJ, my siblings and I to Alabama to visit our family on summer trips. We used to have so much fun. DJ moved to Alabama also.

DJ and I had a great time talking about old times. I also talked to her about how unhappy I was with Rocky and how scared I was to leave him. Nighttime came so I told her I had to go and that I really enjoyed spending time with her. I knew Rocky probably was out looking for me because I had been gone all day and I know he did not know where I was. He was not home when I left and had he been I would not have had the chance to go anywhere. So I knew I had to get home. After I hugged DJ, I told her I'd see her later.

As I pulled off I saw Rocky's Cadillac pulling up behind me. I knew I was in trouble, and I just knew he was going to be angry. He sped up on the side of me and asked that I pull over. Of course I said, "no." He then got in front of me and told me to pull over, so I did. He made me park my car and get in with him and drive. I told him I didn't want to, but he insisted that I drive.

He told me to drive and get on the highway as if we were going to Tuscaloosa. I told him I didn't want to go there and that I wanted to go home. He then started to punch me in the face while I was driving. He told me to shut up and drive, and called me all kinds of names. He punched me so hard he busted my nose. I could not see anything, and blood was everywhere. I told him I needed to pull over because I could no longer see. He said, "Wipe your face and keep driving." I cried while I drove. I begged him to let me pull over as he continued to hit me in the face. He said, "I know you're cheating on me and you know you're supposed to be at home." I told him I was tired of sitting in the house all the time.

The blood on my face was so bad that I couldn't see. I continued to beg him to let me pull over. So he let me pull up in the county store after we crossed over into Tuscaloosa. He said he would drive from there. I knew he was going to beat me some more so I took off running towards the store as soon as I opened the car door. I ran in the store and ran behind the counter screaming, "Help he's going to kill me please call the police!"

The expression on the lady's face when I ran into the store screaming was of complete shock. I ran and tried to hide behind the counter. The blood was all over my face, shirt and hands. Rocky ran in the store right behind me when a guy came from the back of the store and asked him to leave and that he was calling the police. I didn't know what he was planning to do with me but I knew it was not good. He finally turned around and left.

    I then asked to use the phone so I could call home and tell my father what happened so that he could come and get me. He was so angry when he saw my face of course, and Rocky was gone by then. I could just see it in his eyes. I didn't want my father doing anything to get himself into trouble. People that knew my father knew that when he got mad he got real quiet and didn't say anything. Jackie was with Daddy when he came and picked me up. She was also angry when she saw my face. I was embarrassed and thought to myself I should have just stayed home. It had gotten so bad and to the point that I had started to blame myself.

Chapter 10

The Last Straw

December 24, 2003, my sister Jackie had bought a six-pack of wine coolers for my 22nd Birthday; mind you I didn't drink. So I drank half of one, and I was so buzzed and I had so much fun with her and my sister Amanda. We went out and bought me a nice outfit and got my hair done. I had finally looked pretty, and I felt pretty. It had been a long time since I felt this good. I had given up on my looks especially sense I was not allowed to dress up. If I dressed up, Rocky would tear my clothes up or burn them. So I felt there was no need to neither dress up nor buy any clothes. It felt good to dress up, and I thought since it was my birthday it was okay, so I thought.

Anyway he came over and saw me drinking and dressed up. He was so calm so I thought. It was Christmas Eve so he said, "Let's go put Jacob's 4 wheeler together." I said, "Okay." Not thinking anything was wrong I left in my car. We left his car parked at mommy's house. Jackie and mommy lived next door to each other. We got in the car and put the boys in their car seats. He smiled as if everything was okay.

He sped off and drove us to the woods. He pressed the gas and said, "I'll kill you, and if I can't have you no one can." I was puzzled. I told him, "I'm not trying to be with no one else." He slammed on the breaks. He put the car in park, came around on my side and yanked me out. Now, don't forget I'm buzzed from the wine cooler I drank. So, I'm trying to fight back and we were tussling. He ripped my clothes off and said, "You're not supposed to be wearing these kinds of clothes. He told me I looked like a hoe. I fell down and he started to beat me.

I looked up and saw my oldest child trying to climb in the front seat. He saw me crying, and he was screaming, "Daddy please!" It was as if my life had flashed before my eyes. We had childproof locks on the back car doors, so he couldn't get out the back seat. All I could see was Jacob trying to climb out of the front door to get to us. At this point, I no longer could feel any more punches. I was too concerned about getting to my baby. The door was wide open. Traffic was coming from both directions. My biggest fear was not getting beat, and I was scared Jacob would get out of the car and get hit by a car. It was pitch black and there were no streetlights on that highway.

He finally stopped before Jacob got out of the car. I was tired of the madness as I walked back to the car with my clothes all ripped up. I had decided in my head right then and there that I was going to leave. I was done! I couldn't continue putting my children through this. It was not just about me anymore, I had to protect my children. For a while I was scared to leave Rocky, not only because I wanted my children to grow up with both parents in the same house, but If I'd stayed I probably be dead by now, or I be done killed him because there was some nights I thought about getting him before he get me.

At this point, I was tired of getting beaten, or waking up to a gun in my face after he came home drunk from fighting in the clubs, he would come in and blame it on me. I am at home with the kids and I didn't understand why he would say "it was your fault that I got into a fight in the club." or the fact that he hit me in the head with a gun. I felt bad, I wanted to help him so bad but I finally realized I couldn't help him; he had to try to help himself. I had finally reached my breaking point.

Rocky took me from under my parent's wings to his. He taught me how to drive etc. He pretty much raised me. In the past I had made up so many excuses not to leave him. I was also scared of raising two children by myself. I didn't think I could do it. But at this point all I had was God and hope. I started to plan how I was going to leave him. But I knew I would have to leave the state to get away from him because he would just come back and get me like he did.

I planned how I was going to leave because I didn't have the money to leave him at the moment. I planned that when I got my income tax check back I would have enough money to leave him, which was the following month. I filed without him knowing. When it came I left the next morning January 2004. I waited until he went to work. He left at 5:30am. At 5:45am I packed my bags. I realized that all of my clothes were rags because he tore up all of my good clothes. So, I left wearing his clothes.

I left my ring with a note on the dresser to let him know that I was fed up and I was tired, and this had been a rough seven years of my life. I could no longer deal with the madness. I couldn't let my children get hurt. I didn't want them to witness him beating me or maybe even me hurting him because sooner or later it would have come to that point. I didn't want my children to be motherless. I needed them as much as they needed me.

I didn't want to bring them up in that type of environment. Plus, I had become someone who I was not. I was always a happy person, but I became very depressed all the time now, and I had given up on life. Rocky had gotten to the point where he barely touched me, he would go up to two months without even touching me, and he would sleep on the couch. I felt so ugly! He would tell me he didn't want to sleep with me because I was fat. Fed up is what I was!

I called my sister Sarah and told her I'd be there the following day. Of course she didn't believe me because I had said that for a long time now. I told her to pick me up from the Greyhound bus station. I took only the pictures off the walls and my clothes. I left only his pictures. I didn't want the car he bought me nor did I want the furniture. I just wanted out! I finally hitched me a ride to the greyhound bus station. Jesse was so kind enough to take me to the bus station, and I didn't want her to get involved so I told her don't tell him you took me to the greyhound. Jesse and I went to school together. Jesse stayed in my neighborhood, and she was a very down to earth and genuine person.

The bus left Birmingham at 8:00am that morning. I got scared when the bus stopped shortly after it left. "Oh My God" I thought to myself "he found me". However it was just a man trying to catch the bus. As the bus started moving again I started praying to God, "God Please let me make it out of here safely." It was not about me anymore it was about the boys might having to be motherless or fatherless, or both. Leaving them I could not handle the thought of it. Fed up was what I was! Cleveland here I come!

Chapter 11

On Our Way to The Land

January 2004, the bus arrived in Cleveland, Ohio at 7am. The first thing I did was to call my sister Sarah. She and her oldest daughter Mia were surprised and happy. I was extremely happy myself. As I walked outside and saw the snow outside it was so beautiful I felt so at home. I was turning in circles in the snow with my head to the sky and my arms out thanking God, while I waited on Sarah to pick me up. Snowflakes were falling onto my face. I felt like a load was lifted off me, thinking to myself, "I'm free."

Finally free! Tears started running down my face, but they were tears of happiness. Thank you God as I showed Jayden and Jaycob the snow. They never saw snow before. But I felt a little nervous because I was on my own now. So my thoughts were, what's next? "I said to myself, I could go to school." Sarah and Mia couldn't believe I had finally left Rocky. Sarah pulled up to the greyhound. She grabbed me and hugged me really tight. The first thing she said when she saw me was "we got to get your appearance together."

I told her I didn't have any clothes because he had torn up all my good clothes. As we were trying to load my things in to the car Jayden fell in the snow, It was so cute, His little fingers had snow on them he said "cold". As we were drove back to her house Sarah told me that her marriage was on the rocks. They had about 16 years together. Sarah was with Don since she was 16 years old.

So we found out they we were both going through a lot. Were both single and ready to mingle, so we thought. I was hurt so badly, that the last thing on my mind was another relationship. After I left, I was told when Rocky came home from work that afternoon and saw my note he flipped out. I was told Rocky sold our furniture to get money so he could come and kill me and that he was also riding around with my picture on the passenger seat of his car, asking people, "Who took my wife away from me?"

Rocky left two days after I did and instead of going to Cleveland, Ohio Rocky was on his way to Canton Ohio, but his car flipped over in Tennessee. I had nightmares that he was going to come back and kill me. Little did I know I needed counseling bad. I had to sleep with Sarah or Mia some nights just so I would feel safe. I thought when I left I would be happy and okay I signed up for school and started taking prerequisites for Nursing.

I loved helping people so I thought that I would be a great nurse. While in the process of taking my prerequisites. I received my STNA (License State Tested Nurse Assistant). I put the boys in daycare while I went to school everyday. I learned how to hold my own by taking care of myself and taking care and raising two children all at once. This was new to me. I was able to link up and meet with my old friend Kerry. She was done with college, she was a very successful young lady, and who was also closer to God.

I was so happy to see Kerry. I was also able to meet up with Ashley. She had finished nail school, and she was so full of life. I was so happy to see her. I loved being around her. She was doing things I never really did, like clubbing, and partying she was just full of life. Kerry on the other hand, whom I loved being around, she had already done all that I wanted to do. Kerry was more geared towards settling down. I was tied down for years and I did not want to settle down now. It was the least thing I wanted to do. I wanted to have some fun.

So, I found myself hanging with Ashley more. In the meantime no matter what I did I always went to school. I didn't care how tired I was from going out. Every morning, I got up and took Sarah to work then went back home. I got the boys up for day care, and got Sarah's two girls up, Mia and Nia and took the boys off to day care, then dropped the girls off at school. That was the plan Sarah and I had in order for me to not have to catch the bus to school and back.

Chapter 12

Who Am I ?

I was happy! My niece Mia would always do my hair. She was young, but she was good at doing hair. I got my wardrobe up to date too! I was starting to feel beautiful! It had been a long time since I felt that way. But I still had problems. I needed help; I was a broken woman who was damaged and scared.

I needed God and I prayed that he would help me leave, but I stopped praying when I got there (bad move). Little did I know I still needed God! It was very selfish on my end. I was not thinking clearly. I was bitter and miserable because I was still angry inside. I never forgave Rocky so I could not let go of the past. Deep down I hated men, and I didn't want to get close to any man. I got so caught up in the lifestyle of drinking and partying that I was a size eleven when I first got to Cleveland. A couple months later I went down to a size three.

Drinking and partying Sarah and I were going out almost every other night. It felt so good because I started getting attention I never really received before. I was being told that I was beautiful and or sexy, instead of fat and out of shape. I soaked it up like a sponge. It had been a long time since I was told that. I felt so good because when I was drinking I couldn't feel anything. Yes, I was happy partying everyday, but bitter on the inside. I did not want to get close to one single man, but I greeted them with a smile.

I started dating as well as drinking but it was all just for fun, I blocked out my issues that I was not ready to face, or did not know how to deal with. Plus, on top of everything else, I tried to provide for my children all by myself including myself so of course I was bitter. My thoughts were "how can I raise two children when I don't even know how to raise myself" My intentions were bad I became what you called a gold digger. I wouldn't talk to a guy if he couldn't help me financially sometimes not even if they did help me I still wouldn't hang out with them.

Those men didn't even know I couldn't stand them, they had no clue. I was cold and bitter but you couldn't tell because I kept a smile. My boys saw me go out a lot and come in late. Being that I didn't have nice clothes at the beginning of my upbringing, I made sure my boys were ok with clothes, that they had nice clothes, meaning all the name brand clothes. (At that time I didn't understand the principal of being a mother.) I made sure they had that with my financial Aid or my welfare check, which was my only income at the time. I didn't have a clue about being a mother. It wasn't just about the clothes they needed. They needed a mother, which was something I did not know how to do.

It was months before I called Rocky to let him see the boys and talk to them. We met up at Randall Mall at Jeepers. I wanted to meet in public. Of course I was so nervous but Jacob was asking about his father and I felt bad for the kid. So I arranged to meet up there. I thought six months was enough time for him to have moved on. Rocky was happy to see the boys and they were happy to see him. We stayed a few hours so the boys could play with him then we left. I felt a little better letting the boys see their father even though I knew I was done deep down inside.

About two months went by and I asked Rocky if he could buy the boys some coats. I didn't have the money to get them coats. I was going to school full time. Rocky told me that he could not buy them any coats until I come home to him. So I called my cousin Lorenz from Youngstown, Ohio. Lorenz was a great person and he and I were real close. We grew up together. He didn't care for Rocky. I told Lorenz I asked Rocky for the money to get my boys some coats.

I told Lorenz Rocky said he wouldn't buy them unless I came back home to him, and that I should've never left him. My cousin Lorenz said, "fuck that nigga," and brought me the money to get my kids coats and told me not to ask Rocky for anything else. Lorenz was mad about that. In the meantime, I stayed in school and continued to take prerequisites full time. I applied for a job where I did my clinical, and they liked my work so much, that they said if I needed a job after STNA school to come and apply. So I did. In the mist of everything going on, I got a call from Rocky saying he was sentenced to several years in jail. Sad for the boys, that they wouldn't see their dad for years. However it didn't really matter to me because he was not helping with the boys financially because I had left him.

Chapter 13

Reality Check

I started to feel like there was hope with my getting a job because where I did my clinical at the hospital for STNA, they told me I could come back and get a job. So I applied for an STNA job where I did my clinical. I filled out an application. The application asked if I had ever been convicted of a crime or if I had any felonies. Well of course the answer to that was "no". They were not hiring at the time. I was told I should get a call in a few weeks for an interview, I was so happy! Meanwhile, my sister made a deal with me, She said, "take me to work and pick me up from work, and take Mia to school and then take Nia to school. And then pick them up after school" I said okay, After I dropped everyone off to work and to school, I went to school myself.

By the time I got out of school it would be time to pick up Mia and Nia, then pick the boys up but I wouldn't have to pick Sarah up until 11:30 pm because she would work a lot of double shifts. Well one day I went to pick Mia up from school, and her friend asked for a ride home too. I said, "yes," being that she was just a street over. I heard them saying some girl was bullying Nia in school. I felt hurt by this. I thought to myself, "Why? Nia is such a good kid." I got out of the car to go get Nia out of school. Mia and her friend got out of the car as well. I was not thinking anything at the moment just trying to get Nia from school. Mia's friend walked up to the little girl and just slapped her.

I was so shocked I couldn't even move at the time. The girl was so little. When I came to my senses and before I could get to the little girl, the little girl had grabbed Mia's friend by her hair and started punching her in the face. I was even more in shock! I couldn't believe my eyes! I couldn't move! Mia pulled the girl off of her friend. By then, Mia friend started punching the little girl. Then I instantly grabbed her and tried to break it up. Other parents ran over there to help break it up. I was so nervous I didn't know what to do.

I went home scared and nervous, not knowing what would happen, I called Sarah and told her what happened. Sarah said she was leaving work. The police ended up knocking at the door about twenty minutes later. They asked for Mia. I knew they were coming to take her to jail. So I lied and said she was not there I was trying to buy a little time until Sarah got there. The officer asked me to come outside so I did He asked me to sit in the car, not knowing that was just to get me in the car.

I'm not street smart nor have I ever been. So I did thinking we were just going to talk. He asks me to swing my legs around, so I asked why? He said, "you're going to jail." That's when Mia ran out of the house screaming "Please don't take my aunty to jail". They made her get in the car after they asked her who she was. They took her to the Juvenile Detention Center, and took me to jail. They took us to jail before Sarah got home from work. Sarah had to pick the boys up from day care for me.

I spent five miserable days in jail. I made one call home hours after I got there. I called Sarah and told her I was okay. She told me she spoke to Mia and she was okay. They treated us like animals in there. We had to stay in our cells 24 hours each day. I had to wait 72 hours to be charged being that it was a Friday, I had to sit all weekend in that dump. I cried my butt off in there. I was also missing my babies, although I was partying so much I never stayed away from my babies long. If I stayed out late I always made sure that I returned home before they opened their eyes. They would see my face everyday, "reality check."

I had to sleep on a thin cot on the floor because the woman that was in the cell before I came was sleeping on the bed. I was so cold I would ball up in a fetal position trying to stay warm. There was feces all over the walls. I did not have any privacy when we had to use the bathroom. All I could think of was, "I run away from drama to run into more drama". This all felt like a nightmare to me. I thought to myself, Could things get any worse? This can't be happening to me!

The second night my cellmate was released, so, I was in the cell alone. The woman in the cell next to me had smuggled her dope in, and she was smoking and getting high, all kinds of thoughts were going through my head. I really felt like I didn't belong there. I was happy I no longer had to sleep on the floor, my back was starting to hurt pretty badly. I didn't feel comfortable bathing in front of people I didn't know. So, yes, I started reeking by day three.

The food was cold and nasty, and I had no appetite at all, but by that third night I started getting hungry and weak, I was already mentally weak from crying so much. So I forced myself to eat the dried bologna sandwiches, and cold spaghetti. The milk was warm and tasted spoiled. Later that night I ended up getting another cellmate. So I thought that was good especially because I didn't want to sit in that cell by myself anymore all day everyday until I got out.

My new cellmate was big and rough looking. She walked in and said "I'm not sleeping on the floor." I thought to myself, "Angelica you better suck up them damn tears, and toughen up! This big bitch is about to whoop your ass because you're not getting back on that hard and cold floor, we are going to be in here fighting flat out." My back was already hurting, and all I could think was I'm not about to be anybody's punk in here, Hell no! So I lay there and acted as if I didn't even here her ass. The next morning I woke up late because I was finally able to sleep straight through the night because I was not on that hard floor. I woke up and grizzly bear had eaten my fruit cup. I thought to myself, "who eats some one else's food?" I didn't want to even go there with her. So I did not say anything to her.

Anyhow, the fourth night came, the guard walked through the cells calling names, and my name was one of the names called. She than stated we all have court in the morning. I was so happy I didn't know what was going to happen. But I felt like something had to be done. I was just happy to be able to be getting out of that nasty cell. I was hoping Sarah wouldn't be long before coming to get me.

The next early morning we left the West Side women's jail and went downtown to the county jail to sit in the holding cell before court. OMG they gave us Kool Aid and sandwiches after we sat for a minute! I was so happy to drink Kool Aid! I never have been so happy in my life, other than giving birth to my children. So finally my name was called and I was a little nervous going into the courtroom. Due to the fact that I had nothing to do with the fight, and it was my first time ever getting into trouble, I didn't know what to expect. Witnesses stated I tried to break it up. I ended up being released on a personal bond because I was a first time offender. But they put me on probation for a year.

My brother Thomas girlfriend picked me up from downtown, and I ran to her car, she was a sweet heart. She hung around my family a lot. The first song I heard on the radio when I got into her car was "Locked Up." The first thing I did when I was released was I went straight to the day care to see my boys. I missed them so much! I couldn't wait to grab and hold them in my arms. I squeezed them so tight. This shook me up some but not enough. I Still didn't know who I was, and I needed to find my self. I know I didn't want to ever get into any trouble again, ever! Jail was just not for me. This situation was a wake up call for me but I still didn't grow up yet, not all the way anyway.

I was still trying to find myself but still partying at the same time, but not as much as I was. Sometime later on I had to go to court to be sentenced. I found a lawyer through a company that helped pay for my STNA License. They also were giving me allowance for going to school for completing prerequisites for my nursing. They paid for my lawyer as well. My Lawyer suggested that I have some of my professors write letters about what type of person I was. He was hoping that would help me from doing time or catching a felony.

I was nervous about this whole thing. He also suggested that I write a letter to the family apologizing for the whole thing. I did not put my hands on the little girl, and there were witnesses that stated I didn't either and that I tried to break it up. They felt someone should've been held accountable for what happened. The young girl had fractured ribs and a broken nose. I was the adult and my lawyer stated that the prosecutor wanted me to pay since I was the only adult. They felt like I should never have let it get that far. I had no clue that would happen at all. I felt hopeless, like the world was coming down on me. I thought to myself, "I can't go to jail, my kids need me, and I need them." The letters didn't help, I was still looking at a felony, and if I tried fighting the case it was possible I would do 6-18 months in jail if I lost. But my lawyer came up with one last option. He said, "If Mia can come to court and testify that you had no idea that this was going to happen and that you didn't have anything to do with it, you would have a great chance of not receiving a felony."

So I went to Sarah and told her I had a chance of not getting a felony if Mia can come to court and let them know I had nothing to do with what happened to the little girl. My chances would be great at not getting a felony if she did that. Sarah said. "Let me talk to her dad about it." After she spoke to him about it, she said that he said Mia case is over she should have nothing to do with it, She was already sentenced to six months of probation herself and so was her friend. I was really hurt by that, and I was too scared to fight it. I didn't want to take a chance on going to jail and leaving my children. So fighting was not an option for me.

I was so scared to go to court. I had no one to go to court with me, so I went by myself, I cried on my way there, and when I got there. I had no one there to support me. I was thinking to myself, if I get a felony I'm not going to be able to be a nurse. "Everything I was going to school for would be a waste of time." So I took the felony! I was charged with a felony, obstruction of justice because I drove the car away from the scene. I was also sentence to do a year on probation. I was sad but happy I didn't have to do any jail time and I could go home to my kids.

Chapter 14

Get It Together Angelica

I was finally hired at the hospital where I did my STNA clinicals. Almost a year went by, and I had lost a lot of weight. I didn't look sick, I was just small. The weight was falling off of me because I was not really happy with myself on the inside, not eating right and drinking more. The partying became a little boring by this time. I still had not found myself. It was nice to see my friends I had left when I moved south, Kerry and Ashley. Kerry was getting ready to graduate from college. I loved her so much like a sister. I was very proud of her. But we were not on the same page. She was on a higher level than I was.

I was just beginning to grow up, and Kerry had already done everything I was just beginning to do. She was very supportive of anything I did I loved her dearly, she was my best friend. Sadly, I couldn't see that then, I went the opposite way. I was not there for her, but she was always there for me. I would hang out with Ashley more because she was more fun at the time. When Ashley and I would go out I would dance on the floor all night long. I wouldn't dance all night for attention, but; when I danced I felt so free, I felt like all my problems were gone.

Ashley was a great friend. I had a little falling out with Sarah. Everyone has fallouts with their family. So I ended up leaving Sarah house the boys and I. I had nowhere to go, I just wanted to leave that house at the time. Ashley being the friend that she was, told "me you and your kids can sleep here." "However, you can't bring you all clothes in because I run a daycare out my house." The social workers could pop in at anytime. I could not do anything but respect that. Ashley told me, "Angelica you got a couple weeks to stay here and you got to find your own place."

So we slept at Ashley's house but we kept our clothes in the trunk of my car. Two weeks later I found a house, and came up with the deposit and first month's rent, because I was homeless and I had children. I received vouchers from some organizations toward furniture for my house. The furniture was used but it was nice and decent. They gave my children and I beds and couches. I was so grateful for the free furniture. I was finally getting my own place.

Sometimes I would go to concerts with a good friend of mine by the name of Jabar. He was cool, and he knew a lot of people, even celebrities. He would get us in VIP when hip hop artist came in town. He was cool and down to earth and I looked up to him like a big brother. Everybody would go to his house and chill because he was cool with everyone. I ended up joining a dance group by the name of "Lady's Dream." I was able to dance, so I loved it. It would air on TV during the weekdays. I met R&B Artists as well as hip hop Artists. After some of the parties, some of the Artists would try to get the females to go back to the hotel with them.

I was miserable inside but far from gullible, and I was no groupie! I would see women going crazy to be picked to go back to the hotel with some of the artists, and it was sad. I thought to myself I was having fun but this was not me either. I was no Angel, but there is nothing like walking anywhere, being be able to hold your head up knowing you were not passed around nor sleeping with half of the artists, because of who they were. I didn't care about that, I had bigger problems that I was trying to suppress at this time. I still did not know my identity as of yet.

I met a Jamaican man by the name of JP one night leaving the club. We talked over the phone for a minute one-day, and I let him come see me. The boys were gone, and he walked through the house and said, "I could help you get a flat screen TV and some nicer furniture." He said that he had a furniture store. He said that I could work for him and make some good money so I could get some nice furniture.

So I was thinking to myself "My furniture is nice, but I can use some new furniture." So I told him, "I work PRN so I would only be able to work certain days." He said that's okay, "you can still work for me." I was really excited. So JP said he'd have furniture delivered to my house and I'd have to just sign for it. I asked him, why do you have to have it delivered to my house if you have a furniture store. He said, "Because my furniture store is out of town." I thought that was odd but I said okay (red Flag) I was not street smart at all, dumber than a box of rocks.

Anyhow, one day JP asked me to go to New York with him. I was a little nervous but I knew I could use the trip. So I asked him what day, and he said, "tomorrow," He told me that I needed to be ready tonight though because he was pulling out early in the morning. I asked why he couldn't just pick me up in the morning. He said because he would be leaving early in the morning. So, I said, okay and I packed a couple of outfits.

JP came and picked me up later that night. We went to a house that looked like no one stayed there from the outside. When I walked in he had some real big pit bulls. So I was nervous because I am terrified of dogs. He pointed at the bedroom and said go into the bedroom. So I went in the bedroom and sat on the edge of the bed. He came in and starts taking his clothes off and said, "You can't sit on my bed with clothes on." It was a beautiful bed, I never saw a bed like it before. But I still thought to myself, "well damn does he want me to get butt naked?" JP had a large monitor that showed cameras that were on the outside as well as the inside of the house. He goes and gives me a T Shirt and says put this on and sleep in it. So I went and put it on. I thought to myself, He thinks he bout to get some of my hot pocket! Nope!

So I come back and lie on the bottom of the bed and tried to act like I was going to sleep because I had a feeling he wanted sex. He came over there and started kissing on me, and I tell him I'm tired so he would get off me. But he was not trying to hear that. He wrestled me for like 30 minutes before I just gave in. I didn't want to have sex with him, but I guess he was thinking that just because he took me shopping in New York I was obligated to give him sex. At that moment I was turned off. I was thinking no sense of going home now I done gave it up. Might as well continue going. I felt really dirty at the moment.

Morning came, and I get up to take a shower, and get dressed so we could leave. We didn't even leave early like he said we would. JP left to go handle some business, so he told me. About forty-five minutes later he returned. We left on our way to New

York. We met at one of his friend's house. They went off in the back to talk while I sat in the living room waiting on him. Thirty minutes later we ended up leaving, he said we needed to get a room so we could get up and go shopping then hit the road in the morning.

We ended up checking into a hotel. I tried to act tired again. He was not on that at all. Anyhow, morning came and we got up, and got dressed and went shopping. He bought my kids clothes and shoes and bought me some clothes. He also put a nice amount of money in my pocket and told me when I got home to take my boys out to eat and to Dave and Busters and to just keep the rest. So I was okay to have that! So when I came in the door at home, at least I was not empty-handed. At least that's what I thought.

So I started working for JP. I ran and told my sister Sarah I got another job. She thought I was playing, but once she started seeing me with money all the time she asked me where I got all that money. I said, "I told you JP said I could work for his furniture store." She said, "What do you do?" I said, "nothing much really." "He has a furniture store that delivers large boxes to my house and I just sign for them."

JP came later on that night and picked up the boxes then he paid me. Sarah said, "girl that sounds like some illegal stuff." "You should stop working for him it doesn't seem right." I was puzzled. I said, "I never thought I was really working a job it seemed too easy but I was unsure and never questioned him about it." I never looked inside the boxes because I thought it was furniture. I stopped working for him because I could've gone to jail and literally I did not know I was drug trafficking. I had no idea!

My partying became more boring, waking up to hangovers almost everyday. I was beginning to get tired of that lifestyle. My youngest son came up to me one morning and said, "Mom I'm tired of you always leaving at night." He was about 3 years old. I felt bad, that was the best wake up call anyone could have given me. I had to check myself. Later on, I found out Daddy had left Mommy for a younger woman. He told me he love Mommy but he was not in love with her anymore. He said he would never leave home as long as they were raising children together, and he didn't. I was grown when he left. I guess some people just grow apart.

He said he could no longer take care of her, it was beginning to be a bit much. She tried to get him to come home to her but he wouldn't. She ended up moving back to Cleveland. My Mother was also diagnosed with schizophrenia. You wouldn't know she was sick unless you held a conversation with her. Mommy originally moved in with Sarah. Mommy asked me one day if she could stay the weekend with me. I said, "sure Mommy." After the weekend went by, she asked me if she could stay with me for good. She really liked it at my house.

The first thing I could think of was I can't have any fun as far as male company coming over. I told my mother she could stay with me. How could I turn my mother away? Well I would never do that. I couldn't ever! I love her dearly. However, I told her if she spazzes out on me or the kids, or if I feel we were in danger, I would have to get her admitted; not that I wanted to, but I was trying to get her to be on her best behavior. She took great care of my children, better than I did. I would have company come over after I put the kids to bed and before the kids woke up I would make my company leave.

I was a little on the wild side. I was still bitter and not ready for any relationships as of yet. Little did I know moving my mother in with me was the best thing for me. Mommy helped me in so many ways. She was truly a blessing. I was nervous at first because she was ill. But we later became the best of friends. She helped me mentally as well and helped raise my children. She taught me how to be a mother as well.

Chapter 15

Show Time

I joined a modeling and acting agency. I was told I was too short to model, which was okay with me because I always wanted to act. I loved acting when I was younger. I started taking acting classes and doing shows. I would do a lot of Improv shows, which was something I loved. I was told that I was really good at acting. I had a passion for acting. Acting took me to another place, especially when I was on stage.

I later connected with someone and I started doing plays downtown. My first play was "Billy Holiday" of course, and I landed a small part. I had to prove myself. I would go to sleep reading scripts and wake up reading. I practiced getting into my character over and over again all day. I would be in the store running my lines. I would be running them in the car while driving. I got into character so well that even when I was not practicing I was still in character. My goal was to not just learn the lines, but to also master each character. We performed downtown and I was so excited.

I was so excited! I was finally able to do something I loved other than dancing! When I was on stage, it was like it took me to another place. The feeling of making people laugh, or cry and smile it was one of the best feelings in the world. I was portraying someone other than myself. I loved acting with a passion. I nailed my part so well. The next play I landed a major role. Two weeks before we had to do the second play, someone had dropped out. The director said to me, "Angelica I'm going to need you to step up and learn her part as well."

So I ended up doing two major parts for the play. I practiced and practiced and I nailed both parts. I used to love when I looked in the audience and saw my boys and my family especially my brother Thomas, and sister, Kaylee and Sarah. They all never missed a play. Thomas and I were pretty close. He was the funny man in the family. He was good at making everyone laugh, everyone loved being around him.

Thomas is a very supportive brother, everyone can talk to him about anything. Sarah is also supportive, she always had my back no matter what. We were all pretty close but Sarah and I were the closest out of all of us. She was my best friend and also like a mother figure to me as well I love her. Sarah always gives me advice on life. Kaylee was very supportive as well she was my big sister who was also like a mother figure. She was fun and outspoken. Everyone loved being around her. She was the life of the party, and I loved being around her. She taught me how to hand dance, she moved smooth just like Daddy. I loved hearing her sing and dance, and she has a beautiful voice. I was pretty close with Thomas and my brother Jason. Jason was a little firecracker who has a big heart and he's genuine.

Just don't mess with his family because he's known for coming after you if you crossed one of us. Well, all my brothers are like that. Jason was just the smallest but he is a firecracker. I could talk to Jason about anything. My family was at every play. They really believed in me. It felt so good. Everyone cheered and applauded at the end of every play. Everyone greeted me and told me how I nailed both characters. It was a great feeling. I was doing something I loved.

Later, I was an extra in a movie. It was a small part, but it was just nice to have even been a part of it. I believed my shape and my young and innocent face helped me land the part. I was very shapely, and I had the face of a teenager. It was a wonderful feeling to be able to be a part of a movie. So yes, I was very excited! I felt like I was on my way but I knew I had to put in a lot of work. My family was very supportive.

There was still a lot of work that I had to put in to get where I wanted to be. I loved being in shows because it was very uplifting. My family still continued to support me. They made sure they came to all of my shows. I felt love from all of them. When I would see my children, especially in the front row that made me feel even better. My family believed in me as much as I believed in myself. They felt like I was really going to make it now.

Chapter 16

If You Knew Better You Do Better

    I was still acting but it was not paying the bills. I was a single parent. I met this guy by the name of Keith. He was driving down my street one day, and I was outside in the front yard. He had a nice Chrysler 300. Keith was a much older man. He was about forty years old when I met him. I tried looking past the age. Anyhow, Keith bags up and asked me what's my name. I tell him Angelica and gave him my number. He called me within thirty minutes. At this time in my life I was not bitter like I was in the beginning. I was a ready to settle down, but I was still a little stubborn, not to mention I still had not met that someone that made me feel that they would be right for my children and I.

    Keith and I talked for a while and he seemed nice at the time. We hung out for a while at first just he and I. Later on Keith asked if he could meet my children, and that he wanted me to meet his children, and I was okay with that. Everything was okay in the beginning. The boys loved Keith and he loved the boys. We would often do things together as a family. He later told me he had three kids. Well as time went by, children started multiplying. Before it was over with he had about 8 kids (red Flag!). I was upset that he lied to me about how many children he had, but at that time I didn't care because I had started to truly like him.

Keith was into real estate; he liked to buy houses and flip them. He would sell the houses after he fixed them up. I started to see another side of him. He would tell me I shouldn't talk to any man unless he could help my boys and I financially. Of course he would help me out with the boys if needed, but I didn't understand because I thought he and I were forming a relationship. One day, he and I were sitting in the car and someone he knew pulled up. Keith got out the car and start talking to him I didn't know what they were talking about.

All I know was that the guy got in the front seat of the car and asked Keith if he could he talk to me, which is what Keith told me. Of course I was puzzled as to why. But I got in the car and asked the guy what he wanted to speak to me about. The guy handed me one thousand dollars and told me I was beautiful and that he just wanted to talk to me. I instantly thought to myself, "Wow to talk to me for one thousand dollars! Who does that?"

I looked at Keith and he tried to tell me it was okay, but my being naïve, I took the money and put it in my pocket. He then said, " Can you suck my penis, "and pulled it out. I said, "hell no!" By that time, Keith came to the passenger seat and took the money out my pocket and put it into his. The guy asked for his money back, but I told him I didn't have it. Of course I was not going to snitch and say Keith took it. I just told him I didn't have it, which I didn't. Keith had taken his money. So I was looking confused because he had given it to me and Keith had taken it but he didn't know Keith took it.

So Keith had the money but was telling the guy he didn't have it. Keith told the guy, "My girl don't steal," Then he said "Angelica get out of the car and stand up," and I did, but I didn't know why he had me doing that because he had the money. So Keith patted me down to show the guy that I didn't have the money. The guy got mad instantly. He smacked me so hard I didn't even see it coming. I literally saw stars. The next thing I knew was that Keith had back slapped the guy so hard, he flew over the hood of the car. The guy then ran and jumped in his car and pulled off.

I asked Keith to just give him the money back because I didn't want any problems. Keith said, "He could chalk that money now from hitting you." So we drove back around the corner to Keith's house. Thirty minutes later the guy comes back with a gun angry. So Keith's friends ended up making him leave. I was so scared that I just wanted Keith to give him the money back. Keith refused to give it back, and he said he had to pay for hitting me. He said we were going to go do a little shopping with the money.

One night I was out with my brother Jason at a bar on 116th in Buckeye. There was this guy that my brothers Paul and Jason knew. His name was Man. Man was a real nice looking guy. He told my brother Jason, that he would like to talk to me and get to know me. We exchanged numbers. One day he asked if he could he see me and I said "sure." When I met up with him, he pulled up in a black Corvette. I instantly thought to myself, "What does this guy want with me? I'm nobody. I didn't feel like I was good enough for him, nor was I ever on his level. He was wearing minks and gator shoes. I didn't even know what a mink felt like. I had fake cheetah coats. My brother had already told

me he was about his business. I think he really liked me, because he would always ask to see me. But because I didn't feel like I was good enough for him I wouldn't kick it with him at first. But anyhow, we just became good friends and I could talk to him about anything. I would tell him about Keith. He never spoke down on Keith. In fact, he was never the type that spoke down on any man. He would just listen to me pretty much.

Chapter 17

Loyalty Sometimes Get You Nowhere

Keith started to not do so well. The houses were moving slow. I believed his money start running low as well. Me, being the type of woman I was I got food stamps because I worked part time and went to school full time. So we didn't starve. He showed me how to work men for money without having sex with them. He told me all I had to do was talk shit with them. I didn't have to sleep with anyone. Money was really slow for him and I started feeling bad for him.

I felt helpless. I could see the stress in his eyes. He started drinking more and so did I somewhat. So I would get money from other men that liked me and I would go back and give Keith some. (I know, I know pretty stupid, but I was trying to help him, so I thought). I would keep his kids often. I loved his children like they were my own. They would spend plenty of nights with me.

I would say about a month later he finally sold a house. We were all very excited. The kids and I were sitting back waiting on him one morning after he went to sell the house. We planned on going to Cedar Point with some of the money he got from the sale of the house, to show the kids a good time. Well we waited and we waited. He never showed up! I called his phone, and his daughter called his phone. No answer. We started thinking that something was not right. I knew something was not right, I just couldn't put my finger on it. The last thing I thought of was that he did not only play me, but the kids were waiting for him also.

Well to make a long story short Keith was in a long relationship before I came along. From what I heard, she was a hopper. A hopper is a woman that hops from man to man with money. She was only with him for what he could do for her. So I guess she found out he was seeing someone and she canceled that. She felt like someone was in her way, I guess. So she made her way back in his life.

Meanwhile, the morning he received the money for the sold house, we did not hear from him for hours. I started thinking maybe he was with his ex, and as bad as I did not want to think that, I knew something was not right. So nightfall came and still no word from him. His children and my children were sitting up waiting on him, and still nothing. So I called one of my male friends to come and get me for a minute, as I needed to vent. He came and picked me up on his motorcycle. I told the kids that I'd be back. He took me for a ride downtown to the water on his bike. I told him what was going on. He gave me his advice and told me to be strong. We didn't stay long because I needed to get back to the kids.

As we were riding back up Woodland, I saw two people on scooters riding up. My friend John cracks a joke and said, "Look at the scooter kids" and laughs. I laughed with him. As we got closer one of the jackets that was on the scooters looked like Keith's. As we got a little closer I saw that it was Keith's. So I told John follow them but he said that he was not with it, and he was going to take me back home, and that I didn't need to be tripping over that guy. So he took me back home and I told the kids I just saw their dad on a scooter and that he and his ex were riding up Woodland together. They were mad and hurt because we had been waiting on him all day.

    I jumped in my car and drove back down there. I knew she stayed in the projects but I did not know what building. I really wanted to bust his window out but I didn't. I just left a note in the window letting him know I saw him. So I headed back to my house with the kids. Twenty minutes later he pulls up. He didn't even say "sorry" or anything. He just called and told the kids to come down stairs. So they did just that and then he pulled off. I was so hurt and angry about that.

Chapter 18

Moving Forward

I started hanging around my cousin, Diamond, from Youngstown, Ohio. She always had my back, and I'm glad I got close to her. She was like my big sister. She would always give me advice about life and men. If I needed her financially she was there for me as well. I remember a time I didn't have a coat or the money. I had a fall jacket but it was too cold for it at the time. I didn't even ask her, she asked me to ride with her to the mall to get her a few things and I said sure. But when we got there she had bought me a coat and some clothes.

Diamond had the biggest heart and was genuine. I loved her so much. She just wanted what was best for me. Anyhow, one day she called me and said her boyfriend had a friend in town from the west coast and that he was looking for a friend to hang out with. So because I was going through some things with Keith I felt like I could use a new friend. So I told her to give him my number. He ended up calling me later that same day.

I received a call from him later that day. He said, "Hello my name is Dilen, Diamond gave me your number." I said, "Hello I'm Angelica." He said he was in town for a minute and he would be heading out the next day, and that he would like to see me when he come back in town. I said, "That was cool." I was okay with that. We ended up talking over the phones for a minute. He created me an email account so we could email each other back and forth and also exchanged pictures, I was thinking to myself what a nice looking older man. He was older than me by ten years. I didn't know what is was about, older men and me, but I liked talking to older men for some odd reason.

In the meantime Keith started trying to come back into my life. I still had feelings for him but I was trying to hold back. I tried making him jealous by telling him I met a friend from out of town. Although Dilen and I never really met in person only talked over the phone. Dilen and I developed a good friendship. I used to talk to him about Keith. He would give me advice. One time Keith tried to get me to buy an apartment building from him.

The trick was he would give me ten thousand dollars but I would purchase it for sixty five thousand dollars. So I asked Dilen about it being that he was into real estate and he knew the business well. Dilen told me not to do it. Anyhow, I told Keith that Dilen was thinking of coming to visit, and he wanted to stay about a week. I didn't want him to because I still had feelings for Keith, but Keith said to let him come. I looked at him with a puzzled look as to why he would want him to come and see me.

He said I got your heart, and I'm not worried about anything else. I never heard anyone talk like that before. Long story short Keith was still messing with his ex so I found out later that was the reason he wanted me to be occupied so I wouldn't bother him. However, he kept tabs on me. I found out he parked down the street in another car disguised in a baseball cap.

I told Dilen that he could come for a week instead of staying at a hotel, and that he could stay with me and he could sleep on the couch. He asked me what type of neighborhood I stayed in. I told him I was in a rough neighborhood, and that was I off 102nd and Sophia; anyone from Cleveland knew that was the hood. I sent the boys to Canton with their Grandmother so that they were not there when Dilen came. Everyday we did something we enjoyed each other's company. Dilen gave me some money for my bills while he was there. I thought that Dilen was really a nice guy. One day he and I were outside and a young lady from down the street came and told me that Keith was down there in an unknown car watching us with a hat on. I ignored that and I continued enjoying Dilen's company. We had a good time together, and we didn't have sex at all. I thought Dilen was cool, but my heart was still with Keith.

After Dilen left, Keith called, and tried to be nosy about Dilen's stay. He asked what Dilen and I did and all. I told him we had a great time. So, he asked if he could stop by and see me so I said, "Yes, for a minute." He stopped by and asked me to get in the car and talk to him; so I did thinking it was just going to be "a talk." Someone else drove while we were in the back seat. He had a bottle of Tequila, and he asked me if I wanted a drink and I told him "No I don't drink that anymore." Anyhow, the driver pulled into a driveway on miles. So I asked him to take me home. He said, "I want you to come in and see this new house I just bought." He said that he was in the process of fixing it up in order to sell it.

So I went in for a minute and I told him to take me home now! He snatched my phone and said, "You are not going anywhere, you my bitch!" He asked me over and over if I had sex with Dilen and I kept telling him "No." "He acted as if he didn't believe me. So, I tried to get my phone back so I could call my family to come and get me. He wrestled me, and he grabbed me by the throat and pushed me up the stairs. I did not want to go up the stairs, because I didn't know what would happen if I did.

I managed to get the strength from somewhere and pushed him back down the stairs, and he flew into the window. I tried running out the door afterwards, but he caught me by the door and grabbed me by my throat again. He choked me so hard that I passed out on to the couch. I woke up minutes later, and he was sitting on the couch next to me. He grabbed me and dragged me back up the stairs. He ripped my clothes off and started choking me again. All I smelled was liquor seeping out of his pores. I got tired of fighting and I gave up. I passed out.

Morning came, and Keith said, "I'm sorry for last night. You're not supposed to catch feelings for anyone else but me." I looked at Keith with a look like, "You told me I should date." I just wanted him to take me home. When I got home, Mia asked me, "What happened to your neck?" Keith had left his handprint around my neck. At this time, I was done with him! I did not want to deal with him anymore. I was so hurt.

Chapter 19

Found Love

Time went by and I still had not called Dilen. He seemed cool, but there was no real fire between us. Dilen finally ended up calling me asking me what I thought about him moving out here to Cleveland. He said he really liked me, and he wanted to get to know me a little more. I was surprised. He said, "You seem like a good woman, and I would like to get to know you more."

So we continued talking on the phone. I was not dealing with Keith anymore but I still dealt with his children. I loved them, especially his oldest daughter; she was my heart. I would do just about anything for her because I loved her as my own. I would go to the school and check on her from time to time and just be there for her if she needed me, regardless of what went on with her father. Anyhow, a couple months went by and Dilen started coming out to visit me, and we spent more time together. Later on he met my boys. By this time, I started letting go of Keith, I knew it was officially over.

Dilen would fly in from Washington often, and took me to school and picked me up from school. Dilen was definitely a street guy. He was in and out of town quite a bit. I didn't really care I just cared that he made me feel good at the time. I really felt like I finally found true love. Dilen cared about my well being. He made sure I had transportation to get back and forth to work, and the boys had transportation to get back and forth to day care.

We started looking for places to live together. He asked me where I wanted to live. I told him I never really wanted to stay in Cleveland long, and that I always wanted to move to California. He asked me If not Ohio what about Texas? I told him I had never been there, but that we could give it a try. I felt so happy, I finally felt like I found the man for me. I never had a man that cared so much about my kids and I. The boys loved him and he loved them. Finally, a man that cared about my well-being and not just about what's between my legs or what I could do for him. I was in school still and working.

He came to family functions. Things were finally starting to look up for me. Sometimes when Dilen came into the house, he came in with large bags that I thought were clothes, but instead they were bags full of money! I never saw so much money in my life! I did not know what to say! I was speechless! I was kind of nervous, but I felt he had control of the situation. I never questioned him about anything because I felt it was none of my business. I was happy with him and I was finally beginning to get a hold of my life. Life was good!

Chapter 20

The Turnaround

As time went by, I was working at the hospital, and I was told I had to take a flu shot and that it was mandatory. So I took the flu shot. Hours later I get this feeling like I needed to throw up really bad. The last time I felt this way I was pregnant but I knew I was not because my tubes were tied. I had caught a virus. Dilen called me on break and I told him I was sick, and he said that he would be in Cleveland that night and that he'd pick me up from work. I told him I'd see him later.

    Later on after work, he picked me up from work and took me to go get some soup, medicine, and orange juice. We stopped at Burger King for him to meet up with someone. He seemed a little nervous, and I did not know why. He asked me about a car that was sitting outside of Burger King, and I told him I saw it but didn't pay any attention. Again, I'm not street smart so I didn't think anything of it. I got home and doped myself up with medicine, and a few hours later, Dilen picked up my symptoms. So by the middle of the night I was doping him up with medicine.

    Morning came, and it was time for me to go back to work, I was sick but I still went to work. Dilen was sick by that time as well, but he took me to work anyhow. He was a firm believer in going to work and making money. Dilen would always give me advice on ways to manage my money. He pulled up to my job and said, "I'll drop the boys off to day care and I'll see you later." I said, "Ok and I kissed him and got out the car. Afterwards, I waved at him and said, "See you later." I walked in the doors, and felt like I finally met someone good for me. I was very happy.

On my lunch break, I received a call from Dilen, he said, "Hey Baby, I know you love Ice Cream, so I am gonna to bring you some on your lunch break. I also have a surprise for you." I asked him what the surprise was. He said, "You will see when I get there! I smiled from ear to ear, wondering what the surprise could be! My lunch break came, but Dilen never showed, and I received no call, no text, no nothing. That was not normal for him. If he said he was going to do something, he would do it. I was beginning to worry a bit, but thinking at the same time he probably got tied up.

As time went by and it got closer to me getting off of work, I began to worry because there was still no call from Dilen and I knew he didn't move like that. Time came for me to end my shift, and he was still not there, so I really began to worry. I had to catch a ride home. I called Diamond and let her know Dilen didn't pick me up from work and something had to have gone wrong. I started crying, Diamond told me to calm down and that everything would be okay. She came and picked me up and we rode to Youngstown to his best friend's house to let him know.

As we were rode on the freeway, I got a call from Dilen, he said to me, "I'm in jail." I started screaming and crying. Diamond told me to calm down and she grabbed the phone from me. I heard Diamond repeat, "They set you up." Instantly I dropped my head. I felt so bad as to why anyone, would want to set Dilen up. Dilen has a big heart, and wanted to help everybody. Dilen is so strong, and I never saw anything break him. He was so calm on the phone, and he didn't say too much. He told me to stop crying.

As I returned home, I instantly went downtown to register for visitation rights. Diamond gave me five hundred dollars to put on his books. So I went to visit Dilen, and all I could do was cry. You would have thought we were married or something the way I was crying. He looked through the glass and spoke in the phone and said, "I need you to be strong," so I had to try to get myself together. He said that he met with this guy, and he had been wearing a wire for six months every time they met up. I could tell he was upset about the whole thing but he was so strong. Dilen also told me the surprise he had for me. He bought me a new Toyota Camry! He wanted to surprise me with a new car, but he never made it to my job the day he went to jail.

Chapter 21

I'm a Rider

I had to find Dilen a lawyer. I met with the lawyer, and he told me Dilen was facing some years. My heart just dropped, and I thought as soon as I found someone genuine he left. I started thinking, "Forget it, I'm in this for the long haul." I'm going to ride this with him. I started going to court to see what was going on, and meeting up with the lawyer to see what would be the next best move.

The police never released the car to me because they said that they needed to keep it for investigation. So I still had no transportation. I had different men take me downtown to visit him, and of course they would pick me up. They knew I was going downtown to see Dilen, and they were just glad to be in my presence or maybe they thought they had a chance. I really didn't care what they thought, I just needed to get down there for visitation and for court. I didn't care how I got there, I just knew I hated catching the bus. The bus was not an option for me. I did not have the patience to sit and wait on the bus. I did not miss a visit, I was there twice a week.

Time went by, and soon it was time for sentencing, I was downtown waiting for court to start. I met with the lawyer, and he told me what he was looking at. He was a good lawyer but costly. This was when I found out money talks. Dilen walked in to the courtroom, and looked at me and smiled as if nothing's happened. I never saw anything break him before. No matter what, he always smiled. Anyhow, the judge called his name and went over everything that he was being charged with and stated, "Dilen you will be sentenced to six years and four years of probation." My heart dropped. I had a visit scheduled right after court. So I went upstairs to visit him and I'm crying he said, "Stop crying Angelica, everything is going to be alright."

Dilen got sent off to Lorain. He Knew I didn't have a car to get back and forth to come and see him down the road. So, he had someone to wire money into my account so I could buy me a car so that I could have transportation to get back and forth to work and to see him, because the detectives were not going to release the car that he bought for me. So I ended up getting a car, It was not a new car, it was a used Cavalier but it got me from A to Z. I was happy with my little Cavalier. I always liked to surprise him, and pop in on him. I would never tell him when I was coming, I would just show up.

I started working more and I stopped going to school to complete my prerequisites. I only had two more prerequisites to complete but I had to put it on hold. It was time I stepped up my game and put on my big girl panties and start working more so I could take care of my children on my own. I did not want to depend on anyone helping me anymore.

Chapter 22

Time I Get Me Together

In the meantime, several months went by, and I started picking up a lot more shifts at work. I met and got close to a few young ladies at the hospital. One of them was Shane, and she and I had become pretty close. When her car broke down, I picked her up and gave her rides to work or let her drive herself to work. We became as close as sisters. We had a lot in common. One day Shane asked me to go back to school for nursing and I told her I already went and took prerequisites, I just had a couple more to take. She said, "No, I'm talking about doing an accelerated program where we could get our nursing license in twelve to fifteen months." She said, "Now, you know time flies," I told her, ok sounds interesting. I said, "let's check into it."

Shane and I went to the school to see and to check and find out all about the school, and it sounded like a go. So we went to sign up for school. We were told we needed to take an assessment test before we enrolled. So we scheduled an appointment to take the test. Later during the week, I went to take my test and I scored high enough on the math test to not have to take a math class. I failed the reading test. However, failing or passing a test does not determine whether you got into the school or not. The test just allowed them to know where you were and what your strengths and weakness were. So, I had to take a reading class before I went into my nursing class.

Shane and I started going to school together. We had to commute Monday through Friday, thirty miles one way. Shane's car broke down of course, My being a good person, I told her I'd pick her up and we rode together to school. Shane told people that she and I were best friends. The deal we made in the beginning was that we would stick together through nursing school. Some days I would even give her a ride to and from work when she had to work different days than I did. Or I would let her use my car to get to and from work. We were pretty close.

I finished my reading class. Intro to Nursing class began I was excited! Shane and I were in the same class. I met a few other ladies in the Intro to Nursing class, and they were pretty cool. Friday came and we took a test, and as I was taking the test I knew the material, I just didn't understand the questions, and how they were worded. But I still gave it my all, and I had confidence I'd passed the test. I was excited because I had studied hard the last few days. An hour later, the teacher, she grades the tests, and passed them back so we could see our scores.

When she got to my test, she handed it over to me and I saw that I had an "F." I was certain I passed that test. So the next test I studied even harder. By the end of the four weeks, the class was about over. The last day when the teacher gave us our final grades, she called me up, and told me I had failed her class. So now I had to retake the class. I was hurt and mad all at the same time. But giving up was not an option.

The following, week another Intro to Nursing class had started. Everyone in my class was new. It was an accelerated program, and the class only lasted four weeks. The class that I was with before had gone on to the next class, which was Anatomy. I was left behind. At this time, Shane had moved on to the next class. Shane had also bought herself a car, so she began to drive herself to and from school, which was good, because we were going to school at different hours now. We were still talking, but her attitude had sort of changed.

I felt like she did not want to be bothered with me anymore when I would call her. She seemed kind of distant, although I did not know why. I questioned myself as to what I could have done wrong. I loved Shane like she was my blood sister. Word had gotten back to me that she said I called her too much. I felt that was odd but I never questioned her about it. It was like she did sort of change, but I remain positive and went into my class again with a positive attitude. I met some nice young ladies in the class. They were really nice to me. Madison, who was the party animal, had a big heart, she just loved going out and partying. When we wanted to step out for happy hour, Madison would know the place to go.

Camilla was cool and laid back. She had a big heart too, but if you pissed her off, she'd get in your butt. Tiona who was silly as hell she also had a big heart. Camilla and Tiona took school very seriously. We all became pretty close. We started car-pooling together. We were like one big happy family. We all clicked right away. They were like my big sisters. They were over protective of me especially Tiona and Camilla. Tiona had a big heart too. All I kept thinking about were my boys were going to be so proud of me when I finished school, and how I would someday afford to buy a decent house, a nice new car, and move them up out of the hood.

Chapter 23

Grind Time

The first week of school was going by pretty fast. It was Thursday already, and we had a test tomorrow, and I had been studying all week. Friday came, and I was a little nervous, but I still was confidant that I would pass. The teacher graded the tests and passed them back and I still received a low grade. I was so upset, and I did not understand what I was doing wrong. So I waited after class to tell her I don't know why I failed the test because I studied and I know the material, and I was able to explain the material back to her with no problem. She stated, "You sound like you know the material, but maybe you should get checked out to see what's going on." So, I scheduled an appointment to get checked out.

Tuesday came, and after school I went straight to my appointment. I was very concerned to know what was going on with me and why I was having a hard time passing the test to Intro to Nursing. So I got there and talked to the Psychologist and let him know what was going on. He said that he would run some tests on me. After he ran all of the tests, my results were finalized, later that day. He called me back in the office and asked me to sit down. He said, "You have a learning disability." I told him I was never in special classes throughout grade school, so how could I have a learning disability?

I then started thinking that the Cleveland school district just passed me by to get me out of their school. I never passed my proficiency tests in High School. I struggled when taking those tests. I had a hard time passing the English, Math, and Reading tests. After the third try I finally passed the English part, but I never passed the math and the reading. I ended up years later getting my diploma through a company that allowed me to take the work home and complete it and then turn it in a few days later. They printed out my diploma the same day I go to turn in my assignments.

The Psychologist told me he's sorry to tell me but I should sue the school I am attending because there charging me thousands of dollars to attend a school when they should have never let me in the school. I should have never, because I didn't pass the entrance to the reading portion of the test. He said that my comprehension was on a Junior High level, and that there was no way I could learn college material, when I don't know the basic material, and that's why I struggled when taking the tests because I don't understand the questions. I stated that I did my prerequisites at a community college and I passed with no problem.

The psychologist stated that's because that's basic material, and they break the information down for you. He gave me his best friend's card, and told me to call him, and that he was a lawyer and he could help me sue the school. He told me to withdraw from school and to file a lawsuit because I had already signed papers to pay thousands of dollars for nursing school. Before I left his office, he gave me copies of my test results stating I had a problem, and I felt both hopeless and helpless!

As I was walked to my car, I just started crying and thinking how I would tell my family and friends this news. They're going to think I'm stupid, and what would my boys think! I was thinking I'd never become anything. So when I returned home, I told my Mommy that, "They are saying I'm too slow to go to nursing school, so I'm going to quit." Mommy just dropped her head and said, "I wish I could help you through it, but because I never made it to High School, I don't know how to help you." Mommy told me to pray about it, the look on her face was sad and hurt because she really wanted to see me finish school.

She asked me if I could get someone to help me at the school so I wouldn't have to quit. I knew if she could help me she would. She was my best friend and she wanted what was best for me. Sarah was the first person I called. I called her and told her that they said I should quit and go back to community college and start from there because my comprehension was not at a college level. She was in disbelief, and she told me that I could do it, and that I would just need to find a way of studying and to just ask questions if I didn't understand.

I thought to myself I was too slow, and I was not convinced to stay and fight it out and I just wanted to give up. So of course I called Tiona, Camilla, and Madison that I was car-pooling with and told them what was said to me, and that I was dropping out. They all said, "No don't drop out!" Especially Camilla, she was very strong about me not dropping out. They told me to stay in school, and they promised to make a pact to study twice a week with me and to explain anything I didn't understand during class and after class. I loved those ladies so much!

  We all studied together twice a week. Once they started helping me and breaking things down for me, I started understanding a lot more. I started passing my tests! I felt like these girls were my blood family. We studied together and we ate together. Sometimes we even fell asleep studying and slept together. We were in it together. Mommy would cook and have food ready for us everyday we came home from school. She stepped in even more with the boys because I hardly had time for them. I started working PRN instead of full-time at the job because I was in school full-time.

  I didn't have much time to work but had to because I still had bills to pay. Whatever I was short on Mommy stepped in and helped because she was my backbone. She would tell me, "Don't worry all the time." Even when it came to a light bill, if I didn't have the money she would say, "I'll pay it." I felt bad taking her money like that because I knew she was on a fixed income. So, I always told myself when I got out of nursing school I would take great care of her. In the meantime, I'd still go to visit Dilen. Sometimes I couldn't afford to go see him because the car that I bought with the money he gave me was a used car, and had a lot of problems.

  So, I started having to get rentals. I did not have the money to get rentals all the time because I didn't work much, but because I felt like I needed to see him, I had to sometimes I'd sell my food stamps so that I could have enough money to get a rental to go and see him. Of course I wouldn't tell him that's what I did because I didn't want him to feel sorry for me.

One time after I got the rental I think I had about forty dollars to my name. So I would get all day visitation because I would drive three hours there and three hours back. I always tried to make sure I had enough money for the vending machines and for at least one photo.

While we were sitting and talking, I bought him some food from the vending machine. He asked me was I going to get myself something from the vending machine. I told him I was not hungry, but truthfully I was, my stomach was touching my back. So I told him I was cool and that I ate before I came, I was watching him eat those wings, and they were looking and smelling mighty good. Dilen knew that I was not a good liar, so he asked me, "How much money did you bring with you?" I told him I didn't have the money to come, and I had to sell some of my food stamps.

He felt bad and he said, "Why didn't you say something?" I told him I didn't want him to worry. So he said, "I'm going to send you some money." A few days later he had a money order sent to me from prison. Dilen told me he would have money sent to me to help out, and he did. Dilen knew me like the back of his hand. Dilen and I got even closer while he was inside the walls. I asked him for advice about everything, and he would coach me from the inside, especially on how to start saving money and making wise decisions about prioritizing important things in my life, as well as when it came to the boys.

He was always on me about making sure they stay involved with sports. I would keep him updated about everything that was going on on the outside as well. Dilen was always calm about everything even when I told him about my learning disability. I was embarrassed to tell him at first, because I didn't know what he would think about me. But I knew he needed to know, but he never judged me nor made fun of me. He just reassured me that I would get through it, and to just focus and study. He said, " You can do it, and you will be okay."

The only thing I did not tell him because I did not want to hurt him while he was in jail, I started dating later on down the line. But my heart was with Dilen. I only did that as time went by because I had needs. I guess you might look at it as if I was weak but honestly some nights I would get lonely. No matter who I talked to, I always told them about Dilen. If a guy was in my presence when Dilen called me he knew to shut up, and play his role.

Although he was locked up, he was still number one in my book. I never let anyone disrespect him when he called. I loved him too much to let any man disrespect him, especially while he was down. Dilen was my best friend. He knew me more than any man except my father. Dilen was never the type of man that tried to take anything from me. If anything, he would always provide for me.

Meanwhile, months had gone by in school and Camilla, Madison, and Tiona and I we were still rolling together. We were chopping classes down. Every month we would graduate to a new class. Madison started a trend at the end of every final. After finishing her test, Madison would get up and say "bricks," and hand the test over to the teacher and just walk out the class. It was lyrics to a song. That was our cue that we were out of the class and onto the next class. We would do stupid things together like that. People just looked at us like we were crazy, but they wouldn't say we were crazy to our faces.

We all became really close, If one cried we all cried, if one got mad we all got mad. At the end of every month when we completed a class, we would go and have drinks and celebrate. We didn't go out often because we were too busy studying all the time, but if we did go out, we would take our flash cards everywhere we went. We lived and died by flashcards. We would be at Bar B Q's with flash cards, flashing each other. So we took school pretty seriously! At this time I was not speaking to Shane really at all. I heard that she spoke badly about me to some people.

At this point I was numb to the ignorance and I just stayed focus. My friend Shannon, who was also in nursing school with us, was real cool with everyone and she was also real funny. I loved Shannon too. She was like my little sister. Sometimes she would come to the house and study with us. One day Shannon came to me and told me Shane had been talking bad about me and that she told people my business as far as my having a learning disability and that I couldn't comprehend past a Junior High School Level. She told people that I had to cheat in all my classes to pass them. So I was pretty upset about that.

So I called her and asked her if she had a problem to meet me at my house. I was so fed up with her ass. I knew she would probably not come alone. So I called my sister and told her to meet me at my house just in case frog face wanted to try and to jump me. Shane pulled up right after my sister did but she wanted to let her big cousin do her work for her. Anyhow, Sarah told me to get on the porch because she was all mouth so they could leave. Mia ran off the porch because she was doing all that talking and struck at her and called her out to fight but Shane didn't want to fight Mia. Mia is very over protective of me, she acts like she the aunty. She wont let no one disrespect me. I love her that's my little sister/ niece we are very close. They got back in the car and left. Shane's mother was really nice to me all the time. She and her other daughter came over later and apologized to my mother and I for Shane's actions. She didn't like drama. She was one of the most genuine ladies I have ever met. She would always keep it real.

Anyhow, we were getting close to finishing school. I was going through a lot. I found out Jayden had a learning disability as well. Doctors had diagnosed him with ADHD. At first I was in denial, but as time went on, I was called up to the school two to three times a week, so something had to be going on with him. Jayden would climb on the desk all the time, he wouldn't sit still in class, and he would get up out of his seat a lot without permission. His grades were also poor. So I tried to sit down and help him with his homework, and he would always forget what I just went over with him.

It was like Jayden couldn't retain any information. I found myself hollering a lot at him because he kept giving me the wrong answer, and he would cry. When I saw him cry I would cry and feel bad because he really didn't know the answers. I was so frustrated because I felt like I did not have the time to be teaching him, and I needed help. I needed to be studying myself because we were being tested twice a week at school at this point. Jayden needed additional help! The school suggested that I put Jayden in Cleveland public schools because they offered special education classes.

I had Jacob and Jayden in private schools, but they didn't offer special education classes, which was fine with me because I didn't want Jayden in special education classes anyhow. Public schools were their only option since we lived in the hood. Because I had low income, I received scholarships that paid for them to go to private schools. I just had to pay ten percent of three thousand and three hundred dollars a year each. When I was growing up, I felt like children were getting cheated out of their education. They were always going on field trips, and having pizza parties and doing puzzles.

So I had my reason as to why I didn't want them to grow up in special education classes. Things changed over the years, but I did not want to take any chances with my sons. I was so frustrated I would be studying so hard because of my disability I hardly had time to work with him on his assignments. So, I found out about a college downtown; they were offering free tutoring twice a week to children. So I signed him up and started taking him downtown. It helped him, but not like it should of, I guess because it was students teaching him. They didn't have a license, nor did they have a history of experience. It was their way of receiving credits. He still couldn't focus in class. I didn't want to complain about free help, but Jayden needed more help. I later found out about this man by the name of Magic. He would come to your house and tutored your child if they needed it. He was real good with tutoring, and he had several different college degrees as well. The only thing was, that there was a charge, and by me not working often I could not afford it, so I said, "well I'm going to have to sell some food stamps to pay for it because money was very tight." I barely had money to buy Jayden's and Jacobs's shoes while I was in school because I didn't work much. So Magic gave me a monthly package deal and I paid for a month's worth of tutoring for Jayden.

Jayden was in the first grade and he hated reading in front of the class because he didn't know how to read. Magic taught him how to read in a week! He also taught him how to work on other subjects such as math. One day Jayden snuck his book to school and read it in front of the class and they all stood up and clapped after he finished it. The teacher was proud of him and so were the students. I had no idea he had done that until I picked him up from school, and the teacher told me he read a book in front of the class. Jayden started to understand the material that he was struggling with, but he just could not seem to sit still in class and focus; he would be all over the place.

So I took Jayden to see the psychologist who diagnosed him with ADHD. She stated it would be best to put him on medication. I did not want to put my baby on medication that was the last thing I wanted to do. But he would not focus and sit still. She said it would help him stay focused in class. So I felt like I had no choice but to try it and see if it helped. She prescribed Jayden ten milligrams of Adderall. As time went by, I noticed he started doing better in school. Teachers told me he was focusing a lot better, and that they saw changes.

The main thing I hated was that Jayden was a zombie, He was not himself, and I did not like that at all. He would just stare off into space all the time. He hardly talked, and he was just not himself. Jayden hardly had an appetite, and he was very emotional. If you said, "boo," he cried. So I said to myself, As soon as I get finished with school, I'm taking my baby off those meds, so I'll have more time to work with him.

I could finally see the light! I finally made it to the last class of the Nursing Program! I was excited and exhausted all at the same time. I took my finals but I needed a certain grade to pass the class. I was so nervous, and the test was so hard, I was just praying I passed. The teacher went to grade the tests, and after everyone finished, everyone was so nervous because her class was so difficult, and there were a lot of trick questions. After she graded them she started letting everyone know if they passed her class or failed. When she got to me, she told me I failed. If looks could kill she would've been dead! I thought she lied.

I was ready to slap fire up out of her mouth! I wanted out of her class so badly. Well, come to find out, the next person she told also failed the test. So we asked to see our tests. When I saw my test I had failed the test by one point. I read over all the questions that I got wrong to check and see if maybe one of them was right. Aha! I found one that she marked wrong that was actually right!

So I took the test back to her and told her she marked one question wrong, when it was actually right. She said, "No that's wrong! She told me to challenge it and if was in the textbook then I would get the credit for that answer. So I got the textbook out and flipped through the chapter nervous and anxious. "Finally, ha! I found it." So I went to show her that answer was indeed correct. She then gave me my point, and I passed the class. Thank God! This last year had been hell for me.

Chapter 24

You Can and You Will

After all I had gone through to finish, school is finally over! It had been hell, but I did it! Thanks to God and the people he placed in my life. OMG! I was so happy! That was one of the happiest days in my life, other than giving birth to Jayden and Jacob. I had made it! I couldn't wait to get home and share the news with my boys and my family, and to tell Dilen when he called. I loved those ladies that stuck it out with me so much and helped me. My mother, Dilen, and close family and friends believed in me more than I did. I love them all.

The feeling was unexplainable, especially when I was told by a doctor who has a degree and license, that I would not make it through school because my comprehension level was too low, He also told me I wouldn't even pass my nursing boards either. So I believed him, and I almost gave up and quit. He also told me I needed to quit and sue the school for taking my money. Oh, how the tears just rolled down my face, tears of happiness and joy. I couldn't help but jump up and down, scream and thank God. Words couldn't explain how I felt! The girls and I threw a party downtown to celebrate our success of graduating together. We made it hell, sleet and snow, we hung in there together.

My family and friends came and celebrated with us. We had a blast! One of my friends I worked with took me, took me out to dinner to celebrate. I still needed to take my nursing boards. I knew I needed help with that. So I heard about a lady by the name of Stacy, who could help. Stacy prepared everyone for nursing boards. She was the bomb! Future nurses would go to Stacy and take her class and do her toe-to-toe. She would tell you when you were ready to take the test.

Everyone loves Stacy. I shared me catching a case with her in the past and she did not look down on me nor was she judgmental at all towards me. She was a great listener and very understanding. I went to her for a couple of months before I registered to take my test because I was so nervous about taking it. I was more so worried about my not understanding the questions on the test and failing it.

I was embarrassed to tell Stacy, so one day after class I waited until everyone had gone and I went and told her hoping she could give me some advice, and she did. She told me to come to her for a while and do her toe-to-toe and I would be fine, because she breaks down everything that's on the test in her toe to toe as well, and also that you would be ready for Nursing Boards exam. It definitely built my confidence. I also heard positive testimonies every week from other people who saw Stacy for help.

I finally started feeling comfortable with the material so I finally sent my paperwork off to register for boards. In the meantime, I continued to study and go to Stacy's review class. I picked up some shifts at work so I could get caught up and make some money because the boys were in need of clothes and shoes. Mommy was in; grind mode now, and everything else was on freeze. I started spending more time with Jayden, and tried to understand his needs.

I took him off of the Adderall. Of course he didn't know it, but I didn't want my baby taking meds because he was like a zombie. I took the Adderall and put them up. I wanted my baby back! I missed his bubbly personality! So what I did was I went to Walgreens and I bought some Flintstone vitamins. I told Jayden that the doctor had switched his medication and she put him on a something different.

So every morning I would give him a Flintstone vitamin instead. I wanted to see how he was going to act with the change. So the first day I gave him the vitamin he said, "Mommy this medicine tastes good." I laughed and I told him, maybe that's why she switched up so you would like it! A few weeks went by, and one day I was rushing and behind schedule, and I forgot to give him the vitamin. So, when he came home he said, "Mommy you forgot to give me my medicine so I couldn't sit still or focus."

Jayden was trying to warn me because he had gotten in to trouble in class and he tried to blame it on the medicine that he missed that morning, when I already knew he had not had it in three weeks. I couldn't help it but to laugh to myself. Of course, I never told him I had switched and had given him Flintstone Vitamins instead. I just looked at him and shook my head. Come to find out he didn't need to take the medication in the first place. What he needed was my attention and for me to show up at that school if needed and stay on his butt.

I developed a good relationship with his teachers and let them know in front of Jayden that I didn't have any problem coming to the school. After I cleared that up, (oh yes he was scared when I would come to the school because I showed up and showed out when needed.) I was also able to give him more of my time. After that I hardly had any problems with Jayden.

Jaycob, on the other hand, had his ways but not nearly as bad. He was a little more understanding as to what Mommy was trying to do. However Jacob was a little sneaky, but I nipped him in the bud. Jayden and Jacob are decent kids, but I'm not going to say perfect because they are far from perfect but I am learning and teaching them at the same time. They are also learning how to be respectful boys, and how to have morals. I had to learn how to be Mommy *and* Daddy, so with that being said usually the Mommy is the nice one, and the Daddy usually is the firm one. Well in my case, they did not have that, so I had to learn how to juggle between the two.

Meaning, I had to be firm with them so they knew I didn't play, but also not too firm so that they felt comfortable enough to talk to me about anything. Sarah started teaching me and telling me how to communicate with the boys more, and how to raise the boys. She would always tell me to sit them down and talk to them about right and wrong, and my mother would tell me to get them in church and that they needed to be baptized. They both were a blessing in my life. My mother helped me a lot with the boys and with me. What Mommy didn't teach me Sarah, most definitely taught me. Sarah was my big sister, and we were the closest out of everyone else.

Sarah helped mold me into the woman I had became today. Sarah taught me not to use men, to get my own money, and to be an Independent woman, and to always keep the boys first except for GOD. Sarah has always had my back and I have always had hers. I love her because she's definitely someone I look up to. She and Mommy helped me change my whole way of thinking. Sarah was like a mother figure to me, and I'm definitely grateful to have Mommy and Sarah in my life. I have two wonderful women helping me with my boys and teaching me how to raise them.

What more can a woman ask for? I don't know what I would have done without those two ladies helping me. So, yes, learning how to be a single mother was very challenging for me. But I was up for the challenge because I wanted the best for them. I want Jayden and Jacob to be the best they can be! I was finally learning about my boys and they were getting to know a better side of me.

Sad to say it took me a while to start getting my priorities together and trying to be a good mother. But, honestly, some people never get it, so I was just grateful that I had learned my lesson before it was too late. Life was not just about me anymore, I had to make everything evolve around the boys and put them before myself. Everything was starting to not only look up, but also feel better.

In the meantime, my papers came back from the boards stating they couldn't grant me the option to take my nursing boards and become a Nurse because I had a felony. While I was reading that my heart dropped. First thing I could think of was that I did all of this studying and took out all of those loans just to be turned down, because of my felony. When I told the school in the beginning that I had a felony and that it was obstructive justice, they told me it was fine and I could continue applying for school because it didn't have anything to do with violence, drugs, or theft.

Again, the school told me I'd be fine because that felony should have been a misdemeanor. As I continued to read the letter they had scheduled a court date downtown for me to see if I could get it expunged! Well I was thinking years had gone by and I had not been in any trouble, which meant I should be good. I should be able to get my record expunged with no problem.

My court day came and I was afraid to go alone so my friend D that worked with me, she rode with me. D was pretty street smart. We got to the courtroom and everyone that was in there. They were all trying to get their felonies expunged. So D asked one of the women who were sitting in court, as to and how fair the judge was, and is she granting some people felonies. The lady said no, and that she was turning people down. My heart started racing instantly because I just knew she was not going to grant me my expungement. D looked at me and said, "Angelica you are going to need a lawyer." I said, "I think you're right!" Honestly, I didn't have any money to retain a lawyer.

There was a lawyer in the courtroom that seemed pretty good. D said, "Let's try to talk to him and see if he could help us." I said, "good idea, hopefully he will help me because I don't have any money." So we followed him out of the courtroom and asked him about helping us. I said, Excuse me sir, my name is Angelica, I was hoping you could help me with a problem I have. He told me then his name was Larry.

So I went over my case with him and pretty much summed it all up as to what had happened. He looked at me and said, "Wow, they gave you a felony because of that?" I said, "Yes sir." He said, "Give me fifty cents out your pocket." I had a little over fifty cents in my pocket so I gave it to him. He said, "You just retained me. When the judge asks you, did you retain me? You tell her yes!" I said okay happily. He had taken my case but I was still nervous at the same time as to what the outcome would be. This part of my life would determine what would happen with my future! So D and I went back into the courtroom and sat down waiting patiently for the judge to call me.

About five minutes go by, and the Judge calls my name. I'm so nervous I just started praying asking God to help me with this situation. She said, "Would Angelica Carter please step to the podium." I had the bubble guts so bad, I thought I was going to shit on myself. As I walked to the stand, my lawyer meets me there stating, "I, Larry Russell, will be representing Angelica Carter your honor." She then said, "Hello Angelica, have you retained Larry Russell?" I said,

"Hello your Honor, and yes, I have retained Mr. Russell." She said, "Very well." Then she started reading some paper work in front of her, she then asked me a question.

She asked, "Have you ever been in any trouble since you caught this case?" I said, "No ma'am!" She said, "What type of organization do you work for?" I said, "I work at a hospital your honor!" She said, "How long have you been working there?" I said, "it's been some years now, I have been working there ever since I caught the case!" She said, "Have you ever been written up at your place of work, or been on any restrictions since then?" I said, "No ma'am!" She than asked me, "What type of people do you work with?" I said, "I work mostly with elderly and some youth."

She then stated, "you mean to tell me you have been working in a hospital for several years, and you have never gotten into any trouble inside or outside your place of employment, and the boards of nursing asked me to not grant your expungement?" She then said I don't like people telling me what to do in my courtroom! This is my courtroom! There is no reason not to grant you your expungement. She then stamped the paper and said "Expungement Granted!" I instantly started crying and thanking God. I hugged the lawyer and told him "Thank you so much, and I told the judge "Thank You."

I ran to D with tears running down my face, and thanked her for coming with me. I also thanked her for supporting me and convincing me to ask the lawyer to represent me, because if she hadn't I probably would not have known to ask a lawyer to represent me. As we were walking out of the courtroom D said, "Hunny, that was God, and I said, "I know D, you're right!" I couldn't wait to get home and tell my family and friends and to talk to Dilen and let him know what was going on. I kept him informed on what was going on, on the outside at all times.

Dilen had asked me to marry him when he come home, and I told him "yes." Dilen said, he had never had a woman to ride with him as I did, and I had been riding with him and he would be home soon. Dilen said he wanted to spend the rest of his life with the boys and me. He said he wanted us to be a family, and that he wanted to try to get his two girls, who were a few years younger than Jayden and Jaycob and raise them together. I said "Okay I am madly in love with you. You're my soulmate, and my best friend." I felt even though he was gone, he was still here with me. The only difference was, we couldn't have sex.

So when I got my record expunged, I reached back out to the boards to see if they were going to let me take my boards. I felt they had to allow me to take my boards, being that I didn't have a record anymore. Although I don't think they liked the fact that the Judge granted me the expungement because the board then put me on probation for three years. They tried to make it really hard for me, because every job I applied for I had to not only show them paperwork of my being on probation, but I had to give them a copy of the police report of what happened to that little girl. Unfortunately, the report stated that the little girl had a couple of broken bones on her body. That was a day I would always regret, and wish I could change because I would never cause harm to a human being.

Thank God there was a nursing home on Wade Park where I did my clinicals. I did pretty well there and the D.O.N liked my work. My good work ethics finally paid off because the D.O.N. stated that if I ever needed a job to come back and apply and she would make sure I had work. So I went back to Stacy letting her know that I got the approval and was ready to take my test now. I told Stacy I got my record expunged. She said, "Baby girl, congratulations, I knew you would be able to get it expunged!" She hugged me and said, "Now start coming to my toe to toe," and I did. After some time went by, one Saturday I was in her class doing her toe-to-toe, and Stacy said, "Baby you are ready to schedule your appointment." So I scheduled my appointment.

The day before my appointment I was in her class and she went over so much material it was crazy. But by this time I had been going to Stacy for a while now, I was still going even when I was trying to see about getting my record expunged. I still went to her class and I didn't give up, because I was hoping and praying they would expunge my record so I could schedule my test. I had been going to Stacy for so long that I was teaching with her in my head while she was teaching. I felt like I had it down pack but I was still nervous. By this time Camilla and Tiona had taken and passed their tests.

The day before I took my test, Camilla also tested me using my flashcards. Camilla and my Jamaican friend, Luanda, Luanda also went to nursing school with me and she was really nice. We all continued to study together sometimes. Luanda and I became pretty close toward the end of school. She was a very

uplifting and positive person and she would also give me advice on life. She was like a big sister to me and I love her. When Camilla and Tiona had passed me up two classes before the end of the school, I asked Luanda one day if I could ride to school with her and that my car was broken down. I told her I did not have gas money but I could get her a few things off of my stamp card. She said, No I don't want your food stamps Angelica." She then gave me fifty dollars to put in my pocket and told me not to worry about paying her back. I thought that was so sweet and my eyes got teary eyed. I told her thank you, and that I appreciate her.

Camilla really worked hard on quizzing me and getting me ready for my test. She said, "Angelica don't worry you got this." I had the bubble guts all night. Camilla was a ride or die friend most definitely. I love her. I was running to the bathroom all night. The last few days I was dreaming about flash cards because I studied so hard. I also had a friend that I worked with at the hospital who was helping me when I went to work. Her name was Tammy. Tammy was an older woman, but she was very uplifting and she was always in my corner and she always have my back too, I love her. Tammy was a very down to earth and genuine woman who was always there when I needed her. When I would go to work she would go over some of the material with me and she would reassure me that I was going to be fine. Tammy was a very positive woman. Sarah and my whole family were pretty much rooting for me and convincing me that I could do it. Sarah would also quiz me with my flashcards as well! So I had a lot of support when it came to me taking my boards.

The day of the test was here! I went and took the test. I was so nervous I could have just thrown up. I called Camilla as I pulled up and she said, "Don't worry you got this." I called my cousin Sabrina in Alabama and she said a prayer for me. She said I would be fine. As I was walked through the doors I was praying. I got in the room, and the staff went over the rules and regulations. All I heard was the staff saying that I could begin! As I was reading the test I could hear Stacy in my head as if I was in her toe-to-toe class. Some questions I would have to read two or three times to understand the question, but Stacy was still in my head saying, "If you're not sure of the answer do elimination." So I did, and as time went by, I was answering questions, some I knew the answer off hand, and some I had to really think about.

As time went, the instructor said it was time for a break, and said if you choose to work through the break you may do so. I took about a sixty second breather then started back with the test, I just wanted to get it over with. The computer then shut off at number seventy-five. I remembered Stacy saying if it shut off at a certain number you passed. I called Camilla and told her where it shut off at. She started screaming and said, "You passed, you passed!" I asked her, you think so? She said yes! I called Stacy and told her the same thing she said, baby you passed it! I started screaming and crying. I hurried up and called Sarah and the family. Everyone was excited for me, but I had to wait to confirm on the web site. So I waited a few days, then I finally I go on the website, and it said that I had passed. I was finally a nurse! I did it! I couldn't wait to get home to tell Mom and the boys. Mommy was so happy! She said, "My baby a nurse," and hugged me so tight, and told me she was so proud of me. I told Dilen and he was also proud of me.

So now I am a nurse! It was time to start looking for jobs. So I went to the nursing home where I did my clinicals, and I spoke to the D.O.N that promised me a job when I finished school. I went to her with the paper work but I was kind of embarrassed to show her the paperwork and to let her know I was going to be on probation for three years. I did not know if she would judge me or not. As I gave it to her I explained what happened. She looked at me and said, "I'm sorry you had to go through that but, its okay." She did not turn me away nor did she judge me.

The D.O.N said they get people that are on probation often and that she would have to submit a report to the boards every so often letting them know how the person is doing. She also said it's just to keep up with you to make sure you're not getting into any trouble. So she gave me the job and told me I have to come in for a class first, which was orientation. When I left out of there I just knew God was in my corner. Everything was starting to look up for me and was finally falling into place. I became closer to God, and I started believing in myself more. I wanted to be better, I wanted more!

No matter what life throws at you, or if anyone tells you, you can't do or be something. Just know you can do and become whatever your heart desires. You just need to keep God first and believe in yourself and work hard for it, because nothing in life is going to be easy nor will it be just handed over to you. We have to fight for what we want and believe. God and my boys were my biggest motivation. I want to be the best mother for them, and giving up was not an option, especially when I had to look them in their faces every day. So I couldn't allow myself to become a failure and have them witness it. I had to lead by example. My family, Dilen, and close friends were my next motivation because they all pushed me and believed in me, even when sometimes I did not believe in myself.

Dilen would be home soon and we would soon get married and become one. Everything was starting to look up. The boys were doing well in school and now it was time for momma to go and make that money so I could start on our future. Mommy has so many plans for the future Jayden and Jacob. Watch and see!

Made in the USA
Middletown, DE
15 June 2015